THE PASTOR
—AND HIS—
DRAGON

DAN CRAIG

ISBN 978-1-63961-410-3 (paperback)
ISBN 978-1-63961-411-0 (digital)

Christian Faith Publishing, Inc.
832 Park Avenue
Meadville, PA 16335
www.christianfaithpublishing.com

Printed in the United States of America

Hard to believe it's been twenty-five years since the divine encounter with Dan at the Atlanta promise keepers. I soon realized Dan was a broken man on the the edge of total burnout, and the Lord had brought us together for a purpose. I'm amazed and in awe how God will pour out His goodness and mercy on those in desperate need. Dan's book tells the story of a man searching for himself, but also how faithful our God is to answer prayer, especially the prayers of a loving wife, Donna. God restored Dan to be used for His glory and to be a blessing to his family and to a lost world. I rejoice in the part God used me, but it's really about His everlasting faithfulness and love. Dan and Donna are special people fulfilling the call of God. I'm blessed to know them.

—Pastor Mike Mack

It is a joy to see my friend, Reverend Dan Craig, has written a book of what had happened in his early ministry. I am sure as you read this book, you will find these events will perhaps help you in your life struggles.

I will ever be grateful for the help Brother Dan and his wife, Donna, were to us at Victory Fellowship Church in Marietta, Georgia. When they came to the church, I suppose around 2000, they began to work in the church. They remodeled our place of worship. They were also effective teachers. He was a powerful and excited preacher of the Word.

I have found Brother Dan to be an honest and caring person. He always had a burden to help others and walked with the Lord as He was preaching and teaching others. He was admired for this love and care of his family, as well as the church.

I know his book will be a tremendous blessing to you.

—Samuel E. Manus, Pastor
Victory Fellowship Church Inc.
Marietta, Georgia

INTRODUCTION

Today's world challenges people of every walk of life to face obstacles that seem to be insurmountable. Being a bi-vocational minister can often lead to challenges no one can imagine. As a man attempts to hold down a full-time job, a full-time pastorate can demand more of his attention and energy than what he has to deliver with a heavy cost. Not just a physical cost of exhausting the physical body but an even greater claim on the spirituality of today's minister attempting to do God's work while facing today's demands. This is an account of one man's struggle to keep the fine balance between job, homelife, and pastorate.

During my second pastorate, the church was showing signs of distress as membership dwindled, and I seemed to be just going through the motions as a pastor and not a devoted man called of God to shepherd His flock. I had a hard time finding the joy that enveloped me as a young minister many years before. I toyed with the idea that the Lord had all but abandoned me. I felt the blessings of the Lord were no longer upon my church. I could see evidences in almost every aspect of the ministry I once loved and enjoyed.

My job as a facility manager was not going very well either. The financial bottom line was dipping way below the profit level that I was accustomed to. The morale of the men and women who worked with me was dropping as fast as the bottom line. Even the machinery in the facility was breaking down at an alarming rate. Every turn I took seemed to be the same wrong direction. My ability to make decisions was undermined with doubt and trepidation.

I was once noted for my quick action to the needs of those around me, but now it seemed my judgment was impaled by indecisiveness and fear. In other words, I felt as though I was on a merry-go-round and had no chance of getting off. The blessed manager was showing signs of stress and losing ground. I was grasping for things that I once held tight in my grip, but now I no longer could even visualize a possible answer.

My family life was also seeing the results of the strain that was taking its toll on my health and attention away from them. My family seemed more distant than ever before. My son was in college and didn't need the advice that Dad always had for him. My autistic daughter was not developing the way I felt she should, so I planted the fault at my own door. My wife of forty years was concerned and offered to help in any way she could. I only saw this as another sign that I failed to meet her expectations.

I came to realize that I was no longer walking in the blessings of the Lord. I was trying to fix everything myself through my own means. I was leaving God out of the equation and was attempting to be a hero by stepping in and saving the day through my own strength and abilities.

CHAPTER 1

THE FACE OF
THE MONSTER

As we watch the essence of life leave a person, we become compla-
cent with the hope that maybe a miracle will occur and all will turn
out for the better somehow. A person can possess the very effervescence of life one day only to watch it slip away ever so quietly without fanfare or cries of desperation, only a faint gasp of a plea for help
so silent that no one ever hears this as a person's existence fleets away.
We start to actually think to ourselves, *I'm glad it's not happening to
me. I can't imagine what they are going through.*

My name is Reverend Dan Craig, and many years ago I had
the privilege of pastoring a small church in a small rural town in
Missouri. My ministry took a fair amount of my daily tasks. I was
never quite aware that this malignity crept into my life, and I was
helpless to cease its advancement. Many people watched quietly as
I began to die spiritually. The pull of death was gradual yet firm.
No one knew quite what to do to slow the progress of this familiar
disease.

It had begun its descent into my life almost totally unnoticed,
just as it had claimed thousands of pastoral lives before it ever reached
me. Now I sensed it had its steely grip upon my life, and I felt help-

less to resist. Little by little, life seemed to be ebbing from my grasp, and it seemed almost easy to let go and embrace obscurity. I reasoned in my own thoughts that perhaps to let go of life would allow me to breathe a deep sense of relief. To release the grip of my existence would mean I have admitted that I am human and I have finally met my limit of endurance. I was uncertain whether my fragile ego would sustain such a blow as to recognize that I was merely mortal. I wasn't the Superman I pretended to be. In the recesses of my mind, I thought I could beat these thoughts that grew more prominent each day.

The disease was commonly called burnout, stress, overworked, or simply a nervous breakdown. Whatever the title was, I could now place a name to the face of this monster that can take the most able man and reduce him to a lethargic, uncaring individual. This monster makes you believe that it must be easier to give up than to continue enduring the pain of going forward. Your arms ache to be allowed to drop. You often think of the biblical characters Aaron and Hur as they held up the arms of Moses for the mighty cause God laid on his shoulders.

Your mind becomes dull to the needs of those around you. Your heart yearns for relief from the tension that draws life from your innermost being. You know your inner tormentor is getting stronger while you get weaker. The very thing you hate most, weakness, becomes your ally. You begin to see that weakness is to be accepted as a respite for the tensions of life. It's easy to fall into the arms of defeat and no longer struggle. Your mind races to thoughts of embracing some relief at any cost.

Many years ago, I faced this monster for the first time. It was a mild but cool February day when I began to feel the tightening of the Leviathan's talons squeeze around my throat. I had no idea that this entity would seek me of all people to claim as its latest victim. It was quiet, subtle, and easy to accept without your even knowing it has been lurking nearby for quite some time. It took on the persona of a friendly being, which led me to believe it was my friend, and it beckoned me to come closer. I felt comfortable at first. There were times that I had embraced my inner being in an attempt to escape from the pressures of the day. It never rebelled or revolted from my advances but merely bided its time when it could find the chance it waited for so long. It was almost serene in nature, a sense of calming amid the tension of life's demands. Now it had the strength to take a firm hold and pull me toward it.

After many grueling days of struggling with my inner turmoil, which demanded my full mental attention, I found I wanted a time when I could sulk into a self-reflective mode where the only one I cared about was myself. This is better known as a pity party where my inclination was to nurture my worn-out ego by dwelling on all the misgivings my mind could conjure up. I needed to breathe a sigh of relief from the demands of life.

Whenever I thought of my inner dragon, I could sense that he beckoned me into the comfort of his closeness. His grasp was firm but gentle, and at times, it was a welcome recompense from life's pressures. Yes, it was comfortable under the wing of the dragon. Humanity could not see how much I trembled under the weight of the world I built for myself. I reasoned in my soul that he was, in some way, protecting me from the harsh world that sapped my strength and my reasoning powers. I never realized that the torment of my mind was actually the force that made my life ebb slowly away, and once it started, I was powerless to cease its torrential flow.

Being a bi-vocational pastor of a small country church in southwest Missouri had its many challenges and demands. Being a pastor should be one of the most rewarding careers a man should undertake. After all, serving God was supposed to be a privilege and honor. This was a calling to a higher purpose that some men answered with a zest and zeal. My church, Bethpage Bible Church, was established many years before I ever walked through the hallowed doors. They had survived many different young pastors and all the different ideas and plans each brought with them. The congregation was loyal to their little church, and everyone wanted the best course of action to keep it going in the right direction. They were a loving group of people that cared deeply for their pastor and his family. Their expression of devotion for me was demonstrated many times over. They expressed many times their support for the needs of their pastor and his family. It was always a family-like atmosphere at Bethpage. They were known for people helping people. Always ready to work or follow the directions of Pastor Dan, whatever it was.

Since this was a small congregation of less than thirty, it was needful for me to maintain a secular job while pastoring this church that was struggling financially. The church treasury was at an all-time low, and the bills kept coming in. Many times I looked on the financial statements of our little church and thought to myself, *If this church doesn't make a correction in its efforts, it will surely cease to exist.* Little did I realize that someone should have looked at the struggling pastor and come to the realization that the pastor was going bankrupt spiritually. He was giving all he had and seemed that whatever he gave, it never seemed to be enough.

The church had various needs that most of the people of the congregation had no knowledge of. It was always up to the pastor to sort things out and make the proper decisions that may or may not be accepted by the majority. The hard decisions of the pastorate were more demanding than most people could even conceive. There were bills that had to be paid, members' egos that had to be attended to, sermons to be written and delivered, sickness and sinners all screamed for the attention of the pastor. Each time I felt that I delivered the best sermon or teaching of my entire career, I immediately felt the remorse that I had to come up with something better for the next time. It was a vicious cycle that the interior tormentor relished in. He continually reminded me of missing the mark.

Many times after the services were over, my mind would race with questions about my ability to sustain the level of excitement and enthusiasm I delivered in the last service. That is usually when the nagging questions would start to fill my ever-wakening thoughts. Thoughts such as, *Why isn't the church growing as fast as I think it should? What haven't I done to allow the Lord's work to prosper? What more can I do to reach those that have not been reached? What direction should I be leading these people in? Is the message that I present each week relative to where people of this church are?*

My mind darted from one negative thought to the next of things not done or done poorly. I often questioned myself if I was an impostor in my attempts of being a pastor of this church. It seemed that the former pastor of Bethpage had accomplished so much with so little for so long that I reasoned that I must be falling short of the mark of a good pastor. It wasn't that I did not have competent people that could take on more responsibilities, it was that I could not let go of the responsibilities for fear of appearing not in complete control. I convinced myself that the entire church had to revolve around my decisions. I poured more fuel on my internal fire and was not even aware of what I was doing to myself. My guilt was fanning the flames of the inferno within, and the interior dragon squealed in delight.

While being a full-time pastor, it was needful for me to maintain the issues that faced a full-time manager of the business end of the firm I worked for at my secular job. I had felt very confident of my abilities of being a plant manager for many years. But over the course of a few stressful months, my confidence eroded to the point where stress was hounding me day and night. Being manager of a poultry protein conversion plant meant that I had the added responsibility to get products in fresh and get them out quickly while maintaining all the quality attributes that were expected of a good manager. The duties of this job included a fair amount of travel, which took me away from my family on many occasions; it also took me away from my church with its duties that needed my attention.

Things seemed never to get done while I was away. The job was beginning to close in around me. The decisions that I had to make became more laborious with each grinding day. I felt my superiors no longer trusted the keen judgment that I was known for. I felt my subordinates were no longer ready to comply with the commands I had to issue. I began to doubt my own ability to conduct myself in the same manner that brought me this far. In my mind, I perceived that I was always the leader, the guy who had to have all the answers. The man you could count on for advice for a positive input to your complex problem.

Now I became unsure, unsteady, and doubted the confidence I was known for. My decisions came with great hesitation and second-guessing. My hands were not as steady as they once were. My eyes would dart back and forth as though I was looking for the answer in a distant corner. My thoughts raced as though I was looking through a great drawer full of scenarios that I could use to come up with the right solution for the next problem.

My body ached in pain in ways I never experienced before. It was telling me that rest is what it needed, and it was soon demanding I lie down or suffer the soon coming consequences. My mind searched for ways to simplify all the issues of day-to-day survival. The grasp of control of my own life began to slip through my fingers. It seemed as though I was trying to hold onto a rope that had been smeared with grease, and no matter how hard I squeezed, I knew I was about to lose my grip. I felt that I was not able to cry out to anyone because it was up to me to uphold the banner of my family and never admit defeat.

One of the shining lights of my life at this time was my daughter, Lynsey Ann. She always accepted me for who I was and never cared about the vast world around her. She was autistic, so to her, the world was a simple place with simple demands. She was now seventeen years old and had just finished her high school equivalency program. Lynsey was curious as to how she could experience life through the efforts of her mother and father. Donna and I worked hard on gaining knowledge of new technologies that would broaden her horizons of awareness. We worked with her speech therapist, her physical therapist, as well as the many fine educators that often commented about the dedication they could see in Lynsey's parents.

The world of autism is one that did not have a great deal of exploration at that time. It was a new field that researchers were just beginning to develop an interest in. This meant that every time we heard of a new concept, a new breakthrough, my wife—Donna—and I were determined to see if this would help Lynsey gained more of an understanding for her limited view of life. When the therapists relate to us the breakthrough found in brush therapy, we agreed that this may be the next big step in Lynsey's development. This meant that we had to find nylon surgical brushes that did not irritate her skin and then brush her limbs and her torso in just the right manner that "aligned" the nervous system to help her "center down" and concentrate on communication with others. This procedure was followed by joint compressions six to eight times a day every day. We saw remarkable results in using these techniques, as Lynsey developed her communication skills in vast ways over the period of several months.

Lynsey's world was one that needed constant companionship. Her speech was difficult for most people to understand, as she had her own way of communicating as she had developed a system of sounds and gestures over the years to make her wants known. After so many years of almost no speech at all, we were delighted that she communicated in the only way she knew how. This meant that either Donna or I had to be with her at each step of her development. We did not resent spending time with Lynsey, but there were some times we wanted some relief to have away from the constant demands of being a parent.

Most of Donna's family lived on the East Coast, so it was not feasible for us to have someone come and stay with Lynsey as it was possible for her to have a meltdown for any number of reasons. A meltdown could best be explained as a person trying to explain their desires to someone when their speech pattern and mind concepts would not come out of their mouth the way they wanted it to come out. You can imagine how frustrating it must be for a person to look into the eyes of Mom or Dad and not get their point across. After all, it was Mom or Dad that knew you best, and surely they could understand you if nobody could.

When things did not convey as they should, the frustration became so intense that Lynsey would burst into tears and search our faces as to implore us that the thoughts were there, but it was up to us to cross the chasm and make things understandable. It was at these times our hearts felt as though they would rip out of our chests because we could not find a way to help this precious gift of God communicate her simplest of desires.

Even with the great advances we were making with our only daughter, I still felt inadequate as a father. Thoughts of doubt and despair crept into my mind whenever the slightest setback occurred. I always felt Lynsey's development depended on my ability to under-stand the ever-changing world of autism. Each time we conquered a need on Lynsey's behalf in some area, we came to the realization there was so much more to learn. It was during this time when you feel inadequate as a parent. You begin to doubt your awareness as a good parent.

Those seeds of doubt were watered and grew voraciously with every negative thought I sent it. My internal demon fed upon these thoughts and wanted nothing more than to grow in strength and power to control my every thought. My image of a knight in shining amour was not as bright as it once was. I could see that the shining armor of this knight was beginning to dull and rust. It would only be a matter of time when I could not slay the dragon that was devouring my self-confidence, but he may be able to devour me.

I now realize this is where the monster lived, in the mind of uncertainty of any person. The doubt of a proud man is what it fed upon. Now it could raise its head and come alive to feed off the doubts and fears I have cultivated as my own. The greater my indecision, the stronger it took hold of my life. I could actually feel him arch his back and stretch his arms as he gained more strength, and my uncertainty grew more profound.

Life, to me, was a matter of slaying dragons. When a formable foe would begin to challenge my abilities, I was always ready to pick up the sword and do battle with my adversary. I relished the thought of testing my skills against any new task. I always felt that if I could conquer the next dragon, those that knew me would hold me in higher esteem. The ego inside of me demanded higher goals with each new horizon. My internal dragon was one that I personally built with pride and ego. He was built strong and fortified with long life, as I had seen to each detail of his development. He knew each area of weakness I possessed and would use these weaknesses against me when the time came. I found that the more I fed the dragon of my ego, the stronger he grew and the more he demanded.

Another highlight of my existence at this time was my son, Dan Jr. He was often described as the exact image of his father in many ways, which made me feel as proud as a parent could feel. Dan and his wife, Sandy, were living on campus of John Brown University along with their new son, Daniel Craig III. Dan Jr. was glad to be in college at this time; along with being a newly married family man, he attempted to maintain a full class load while, at the same time, working outside his home as a contractor to make ends meet. This struggle was, in some way, to achieve the mark that he felt his dad would be proud of. After all, his dad made it through college and was married during the early days of his marriage.

He wanted to be just like his dad and handle multiple tasks and still go through life with a smile on his face. His young family depended on him to make the grade so they could obtain the life they desired. Dan was a goal setter, just as his dad had taught him. He wanted to achieve the highest grade point average he could and still work a secular job to provide for his own family. It bothered him whenever he had to hint to his father that he was running low on funds and needed a little help from time to time. Dan took many odd jobs on and around campus that suited his skills as a carpenter, concrete finisher, or electrician. Many times he called his dad to ask advice about how something could be handled that he hadn't run into before. I was always eager and happy that my son asked for advice and wanted my input in to his early development.

When Dan did not have a construction job to complete, he also doubled as a watchman for the campus, which enabled him to get much needed studying done while being away from his young family. It appeared that some of my inner struggle to achieve slipped into the one I love so very much. Grades suffer when you try to work eighteen hours a day out of every twenty-four.

All this activity seemed to be having some noticeable strain on his relationship with his new bride as well as his grade point average. On many weekends, Dan and his wife, Sandy, would come to our home and ask if we would watch Daniel for a few days while they tended to their own lives, and the struggles associated with life on campus. Donna and I were always eager to take Daniel and wave goodbye to his parents, so we could lavish as much love and attention on this most beautiful baby boy as two new grandparents could. It seemed that whenever Daniel was in my arms, the struggles of life seemed so distant that I forgot that they were even a part of my existence.

Finances were always an issue with young college students and even more so with a young family in college. Dan would not allow himself the luxury of asking Mom and Dad for financial help during this pressing time. Yet somehow, as I watched from a distance, I felt responsible for his struggles. I felt I should be doing more to see that his success was within his grasp. What could I do to help him achieve the same measure of success that I had while I was in college? How could I help my grandson's father? Was I truly responsible for his difficulties while he attempted to make the grade? I began to feel his pain and the strain of his life began to sharpen its claws on my insides. Again I felt helpless to express my love to those that meant the most to me. I wanted to let my son know that I was willing and able to assist him in any way I could. But my exterior only expressed that I was in control of my life, and perhaps you should be in control of your own. My son did not want to show his dad his armor was tarnished with doubt and fear of failure. My son was just like me...

During this time, Donna and I were in the completion stage of constructing our new home. It took us several years to dream of a house that reflected both our talents and tastes, but we were successful. The newly constructed house was the culmination of our entire family. Donna gave the Lord credit for the basic design of this beautiful abode. She related that the Lord had wakened her one night and allowed her to clearly see the overall plans and how to get them accomplished.

This was a 3,500-square-foot house that looked as though it was built during the turn of the century by skilled craftsmen of that era. The extreme concentration to details was something that we paid careful attention to. Many long hours were spent planning on how the new home was to look and how we expected to live out our days after retiring from my career over the next twenty years. The nine months spent on getting this place ready for occupancy as a labor of love and devotion to a dream.

Many days after I had worked a full day at the office, I would go directly to the construction site and work another eight hours on the house of our dreams. Donna and Lynsey would bring my dinner, and we would sit around and talk about how things were going to be once we came to this house and call it home. With each step of construction, we got closer to our dream becoming a reality.

On more than one occasion, Donna would mention that it seemed that I was trying to do too much. I would then comment that if she could find someone to complete the tasks I was accomplishing with the same quality I was completing them, I would hire them. Truly my ego was stronger than my common sense. I lent my skills as a man with a mission. I felt that the more I did, the sooner I could relax and enjoy the fruits of my labor.

Even after we finally moved into our new home, there was always something that needed to be completed. Closets needed shelves, trim work needed to be installed, and the spare room needed flooring, all of which called for my time; they were persistent and wanted it now, not later. Just like many first-time builders of their first house, we were running low on funds. This meant that much of the work would have to be completed by our family. We approached these tasks as challenges that were meant to unify our family. Donna would mix the mortar, Lynsey would bring me the tiles from the opened boxes, while I placed each one in place. Every day, there was another project that needed to be done.

The pressures of life do not stop just because you feel too tired, or you don't want to deal with anything else. They will demand your attention whenever they want and have no regard for your mental awareness, your schedule, or your time. So while at our new home, the phone calls kept coming in, asking for the boss or Pastor Dan or Dad. My wife was caught directly in the middle of it all. She had to watch as I ran from the demands of the job to the demands at school to the demands of the church. It seemed that whenever there was a brief respite, a new demand was lurking around the corner, waiting for me to dare take a deep breath. If the dragon could only keep me winded, it had a chance to keep me down long enough to win the battle.

The dinner table was one time when my wife thought I could be solely hers for a fleeting moment. She would always make meals that she felt expressed her desire to please the man she loved and cared about. Donna paid special attention to my comments about what I especially liked about her cooking. She would then wait for the opportunity to demonstrate her love for me by preparing a meal that was worthy of her hero that seemed tireless. Sunday meals were always special, as Pastor Dan waited until the services were done for the entire day before I could sit down quietly and enjoy my family. This was the time we could languish and talk freely of the past week and make plans for the upcoming week. It was a respite of the daily tasks and demands of a busy young couple trying their best to get ahead.

One Sunday evening while just sitting down at the table after church services, the phone rang to interrupt our only relief of activity for the entire day. The guard at the facility I managed called to tell me that there was a major problem there that needed my full attention. My mind raced to the conclusion that if I did not tackle this problem, every person in my employ would not be able to work the next day. The plan needed the input of the boss, as no one else had the answer to this problem. I placed the phone on the receiver and dashed out the door to slay another dragon at the cost of my family. I was not aware of Donna's pleading to allow someone else to handle this one problem. She had no concern for the special dinner, only the welfare of her hero that was showing signs of stress that was making itself known by large blotches of redness on my face and neck. Seeing the concern on her face added to the many thoughts that raced through my mind as I looked into her eyes and said, "I'll be back as soon as I can. Don't hold dinner for me. I'll eat something later when I return."

Several hours later I would drag myself home with no thought to nourish my body with food, only to fall into bed but was too restless to sleep. My body wanted to stop, but my mind would not disengage to allow my body to rejuvenate itself. Tossing throughout the night would cause Donna's rest to be elusive also. Not only did she have to watch me be slowly devoured by the dragon within me, but now he was after her as well.

Donna watched as the toll of these demands slowly took over sound judgment and simple reasoning. These demands were sapping the life from her hero. Donna's sleep was being robbed as well as her contentment. Doubts seemed to creep into her thoughts as well. Were the demands of this big house worth the cost to her husband's well-being? What could she do to take some of the burden from her mate? Would Dan allow anyone else to share the responsibility that he relished? Was he too egotistical to ask for much-needed help? When would he stop? Just how much could he take?

Donna did her best to try and discuss some of the issues she could see me facing. But the wrenching within me kept me from seeing this act of concern. I felt that by discussing my shortcomings, I was diminishing myself and failing to keep my end of the marriage vows. It's always difficult to see clearly when you're clouded by pride. If I had explained these tearing demands inside, I just knew she would think me weak. This was the same young woman I had always tried to impress with my many feats of strength and endurance.

I had no clue that I was not the young lad of my youth anymore; I still believed that immortality was mine to hold on to. Donna's kindness and concerns were now being wasted on a man that could no longer see clearly because the talons of the internal dragon had buried its claws deep into my psyche. I no longer possessed the ability to reason clearly; now I could only deal with the struggle raging within and not my own preservation. I was not aware of just how much more I could physically endure. But I knew that I would be tested even further, as my entire life was being beaten down hour by unrelenting hour.

CHAPTER 2

— ❧ —

THE NOOSE BEGINS TO TIGHTEN

For several months, our church planned on sending me to the pastors conference in Atlanta, Georgia, given by the Promise Keepers. I heard about it quite by accident. I was a pastor willing to give back to the community, so I volunteered to speak at a local nursing home.

When I arrived at the facility, I was surprised to find another minister was also scheduled, and I somehow got the date mixed up (one more thing that was not going right). The young Pastor Steve and I were amused about the situation and compromised that one of us would preach and the other would lead the music. It was a real blessing for the people not to have to hear me sing. I waited my turn and delivered a short sermon on the value of not giving up at any cost. This seemed appropriate to those that were facing the autumn of their years here on Earth.

After the service, Pastor Steve asked if I was going to the pastors conference in Atlanta, Georgia, next spring. I remarked I had not even heard that there was going to be such an event. He requested that I give it much prayer because he also was a bi-vocational pastor and did not have the resources to get to it by himself and would greatly appreciate it if we could share some expenses. It was quite evident that he was looking for the fellowship of another pastor to share this event with. We exchanged cards and left to go to our separate homes and lives.

Sometime later, Pastor Steve called my office and began to inquire if the Lord had laid it on my heart to go. I could see the need of this young man just starting out, and he could use the input of someone who has been farther down the road. There was also the opportunity to enrich my ministry by helping someone else. So I accepted his offer and agreed to make the arrangements for both of us, as I was somewhat familiar with Atlanta. My secular job required me to travel to the Atlanta area at least four times a year on business. So to make these arrangements was not a major challenge for me.

The next Sunday, I told my church of my decision to take this trip to Atlanta and help another fellow minister with the expenses of the trip. As soon as they heard it, they immediately offered to pay all the expenses and wished me Godspeed on this important sabbatical for Pastor Dan. My heart was soaring for this great undertaking by the membership that I came to love as my family. Truly they wanted to show their endorsement and support for their pastor and invest in the life of another minister. This was just another demonstration of the heart of these fine people that wanted the best for the man that God sent them to fill the need of their church.

As the months rolled by, my secular job was becoming more and more intense and demanding. Personnel needed more attention than usual, the machinery wasn't cooperating either, and the bottom line was going south at a swift rate. It was clear that some forces were at work at this place. Whatever these forces were, it was quite evident that they clearly did not want me to attend or even think about going to this event. My prayer life suffered, as I wanted to share with God my desire to go; but somehow every time I began to pray, something pulled me away from my quiet time with the Lord. The demands of a busy life were shouting louder than ever, and they would not be put off any longer: they demanded my attention now. Things began to be a soft blur as one demand overshadowed the previous one. They never stopped, and grew in intensity with each day as the event neared.

As the time to begin planning to travel to Atlanta approached, the problems began to spring up in rapid succession. First, the young pastor called and said he had to back out due to too many time demands on his schedule. I explained that the expenses would be taken care of if that would persuade him to go. He just stated that it was impossible for him to leave at this time. Although his apology was sincere, I felt extremely let down as though I was hit in the stomach. After all, this was his idea to start with. He was the promoter; what if I couldn't get a room now that there was only one of us going? He said one of the main benefits was the camaraderie we would share, as this was a new experience for both of us.

The word *betrayal* began to creep into my thoughts. I really wanted to find a cordial way to bow out of this venture without alarming my family and not offending my church. Although my body and spirit were failing fast, my personality wouldn't let me accept the disappointment to those who expected so much from me. Depression and remorse were standing close by, waiting their turn to have their way with my mind also. The familiar gnawing feeling began to turn within me once again. It began to raise its head and make its presence known. This was no time for my inner demon to be dormant; he was watching me grow weaker and less confident in decision-making, yet I was compelled to go ahead and make the necessary plans to attend this conference that I was not sure would benefit me.

My mind only thought of the things this adventure would cost me in lost time and efforts at work, at the church, and at my home. My mind was filled doubt, remorse, and anxiety. On one hand I was filling a need of my church to uphold their pastor, but on the other hand, I was running out on my family and my job as manager of a facility. I thought that with all the things I left undone, that I really didn't deserve time away from these burdens I placed on myself. I went ahead and arranged all the travel plans just as I had done a dozen times before. Airline tickets, hotel room, shuttle schedules, event tickets, etc.

When the plane tickets arrived a few days before my flight, they were all wrong. The times were not what I had asked for, but they could work if I could stand the inconvenience of early rising and longer layovers. Once again, something turned sour before my very eyes. I felt that I was losing all my abilities to accomplish even the smallest details such as making the proper airline reservations. This was greatly enhanced due to the fact that I traveled to Atlanta on a regular basis for the firm I worked for on a routine basis. I should have known the flights, the airlines, and the times needed for the layover that would allow enough time to make connections. I allowed my ego to get the best of myself as no one else could do. The beast within my being was stealing my strength and growing more dominant in its behavior. I felt the inner dragon subtly growl as if it were gleeful, as I failed once again.

As the time of departure quickly approached for me to go on my retreat, I found the intensity of problems arose at an even more alarming rate than normal. My body was showing the signs of great stress. Huge red blotches began to appear on my face and neck. Sleep evaded me with an even greater intensity. My mind would not allow me to find the rest I so very much needed. The agitation increased with every waking moment of my existence.

Even during the Sunday morning service, my congregation asked about my health and well-being. I looked tired, pale, and rundown to the point my shoulders no longer stood proud but slumped forward as though a great strain was upon them. Their inquiries only brought forth my inner ego to lie and state that everything was all right, and the things that weren't would sort themselves out eventually. I commented that I felt the need to stay at home that week and not attend the Pastor's Conference in Atlanta. The kind folks of my congregation would not hear of it. Each one stated that they were there to support their pastor, and this was the best thing I could do for my family, my church, and myself. Once again, I felt that I was imprisoned by my duty to others.

My darling wife requested that I see a doctor the next day, which was Monday. I half-heartily agreed and drove off to work as early as always. It was always my contention that I should be the first one to arrive at work to set the course for the rest of my staff each week. This week, something was different about their leader; he did not demonstrate his usual pizzazz for life. His enthusiasm was absent. My coworkers showed great concern, as they questioned me about my health, my thoughts, and my concerns. I felt trapped in a situation that I never had before. I was allowing others to see that I was merely human and was about at the end of my rope.

Finally, my close friend and assistant, Chris Karleskint, who worked beside me for many years, asked me what was wrong. He commented that I did not seem to be the same vivacious person that he knew me to be. I commented that I was just tired and worn out. I had no drive left, no vision, and very little reason to see any difference I could make in anything I did. The expression of concern across his face penetrated my very inner being, as we both knew that I was lying and screaming inside for help. But pride would not let either of us admit that I was losing the battle at a rapid rate. My life was ebbing, and he knew it; but he remained helpless to assist me regaining ground that I lost just as many others that loved me. I could see the compassion in his eyes desiring to help, but at a loss as to what steps needed to be taken for his boss and friend.

The crises at work never take a holiday; they just kept marching into my office and demanding more, more, and even more of my time, talents, and ambition. There was never any time to allow my mind to rest or even take a break from the demands all around me. The phone was another source of distraction, constantly calling me back to my desk and giving me the ultimatum, *Answer me, or be annoyed even more.*

It appeared that everything in the office knew just how to get me. My concentration was almost nonexistent. Memos demanded time, letters needed to be written, personnel need answers—it never stopped. Issues arose to new heights. The facility equipment wasn't running right: there were safety issues, personnel problems, customers' demands, and a host of managerial problems. Even my computer would not cooperate by sending emails and reports properly. It seemed that the entire world was now lashing out to beat me into submission. The throbbing within my head told me that my blood pressure was on the rise and would soon need attention as well.

My entire staff knew that I would be away from the offices for a few days, therefore they demanded that I deal with issues that could not wait until my return; they needed to be dealt with right now. These calamities had to be dealt with right now, and there was no one else that could deal with these problems. It was a longer-than-usual day for me, as time seemed to slip by without my even looking up at the clock. There was no opportunity to step away from my desk to eat lunch, but just drink another cup of coffee and bury myself back into problem-solving. The only way I knew it was time to go home was the fact that the rest of my staff had already left for the day and the sun had been down for several hours. I was finally alone, and my thoughts developed into self-pity. I was drained of all stamina and strength. My mind and willpower were exhausted beyond former point.

When I arrived home, it was quite evident that I was tired, late, and totally unprepared to be leaving for a trip the next morning to Atlanta. Out of genuine concern, my wife asked if I had the opportunity to call the doctor for an appointment regarding the blotches, which had now spread over major portions of my anatomy. That was the last straw: I was reminded of one more thing I did not accomplish correctly. With all the reports, duties, and things that demanded my attention, I totally forgot my promise to the one person that only wanted to help me rectify one problem in my life. In my mind, she had pointed out the last flaw of my character: that I couldn't accomplish a simple request by my wife, the love of my life, that was genuinely concerned for her husband.

I could not face the reality of failing at another issue of my life; I simply dropped my head and turned around and walked out the door, not saying anything. I no longer possessed the ability to answer any of her questions of concern or reasoning. Walking to my truck, I did not know what was going to happen, where I was going, or anything relative to the time I would be gone. I simply wanted to *quit*. Quit everything. Unplug. Diminish into obscurity. I wanted to find someplace where I could seek a simple moment when no one would demand anything of me. I didn't want to be the boss, the pastor, the husband, not even the dad. I needed to find some solitude that would allow me to lay down my armor and take a breath of fresh air. But the dragon within had other thoughts. It was his time to take over rational thoughts and implant his own devious plot. I could sense my loss of life and his triumph over my reality.

My truck cab became somewhat of a sanctuary for me. There were no phones, and it gave me the freedom to drift wherever I wanted to go. But I still lacked direction, as my mind wandered aimlessly. I could no longer focus my thoughts into a rational sequence. So I drove for quite some time when I thought of my son and his seemingly simple life on the campus of the John Brown University. So I made my way to a payphone and called him to say that I felt like talking to someone and asked if I could come over. If I could just talk to some familiar voice that didn't want me to do anything, I could relax for a while.

This is something I never did before, so he was somewhat taken back when I called him. He eagerly agreed and said he would be happy to talk with me. My mind began to have a vision of sitting down with my son and talking about his needs and cares and forgetting about my own. I thought of playing with my grandson and acting like a child myself to escape from the cares of the world for a brief amount of time. My heartache subsided, as my mind toyed with the idea of relaxing from the world. I no longer even scratched at the blotches that was now covering my neck and chest. They were a constant reminder that my body was rebelling against all that I put it through.

When I arrived at my son's small apartment, I didn't see the familiar car in the driveway, and my heart began to pound deep inside as depression and disappointment crept in with a new sense of urgency. I could actually feel the presence of my internal dragon begin to rise in strength. His scaly claws now stretched forth into my throat as if to stifle my airway.

My heart throbbed within my chest as I began to get closer to the front door. The pounding within my ears was rising to a deafening thud as I realized I was losing control. I made it to the door and knocked. No answer. I knocked again, and still no answer. My demon now had the upper hand and roared with delight. He arched his back to let me know that he was in charge of my thoughts and my breathing. Shallow breaths are all I could muster as the sound of the knocking ceased and nothing stirred from within his apartment. I was crushed beyond my ability to withstand it. Tears flowed easily now. I no longer had control over my own sobbing, which is something that I could hold back even during the hardest of times.

How could this be happening? What more could I have done? Was my request to much for him to acknowledge? I left a simple note on the door on the back of one of my business cards as if this was another sales call or appointment I made, "Sorry, I missed you. Love, Dad." I got back into my truck and drove off with the feeling that one more disappointment allowed my inner dragon to gain more strength and more control. Tears dropped into my lap as I drove away. My emotions forced my mind to think of betrayal, of being alone, and no one caring. Couldn't anyone hear the screams from a dying man?

As I drove, I wondered if my son realized the pain his father was in. If he only knew what it meant to me to hug him at this point in my life. I needed the balm of human touch to bring me back to reality. Now I was alone once again, driving back into obscurity. My mind began to play tricks on me as the dragon snarled deep within. That's when I thought that I heard a low guttural laughter come from within my inner spirit because the dragon knew I was against the last rope and was about to go down for the count.

Driving aimlessly, the fog of doubtfulness kept me from thinking clearly. I did not know which way to turn; should I go north or south? East may be a good direction, but so was west. Eventually I found myself pulling into the lot of my small country church. A place where I could find solace and quietness I so longed for. I decided that I needed to be alone with God to ask why I had to suffer such great pains. Why I was surrounded by people, yet I felt so alone? Had the Lord himself forgotten me? Could it be that God was done with me and turned His back on me, and my usefulness was finally at its end?

A gentle snow had just begun to fall as I pulled into the yard of the church. Perhaps here I could find the peace that had been eluding me for so very long. This February night made this small country church feel even more cold and dark, but quiet and peaceful. I sat in the first pew and stared at the floor and contemplated all the events over the last few hours. My mind wanted serenity. My body ached for rest, but my soul was as restless as ever. The torment was about to intensify to see if it could break my hold on reality. I felt my interior beast stretch forth and roar, which further clouded my thoughts. It was hard to think rationally as the claws tore at my heart and lungs. I could feel the blood coursing and my breaths getting shallower, but I was helpless to tame this beast that now had the upper hand and was not about to lie still for me to take back control.

I spent quite a bit of time there searching to hear from God, but I knew that the answers to all my mixed emotions would not come this night, as my mind would only drift from one thought to the next without any reasoning. Now I felt that I had let God down as a minister. How could I call myself His servant when I couldn't even hear from Him in his own house? Tears fell onto the floor of the sanctified house of God. I wondered if He was there anymore. This was the final blow. My mind felt as if God had forsaken me. This was more than I could accept. There was nothing left for me in the house of God. I was not only empty but I was totally alone.

As I locked the front door, my thoughts turned to my close friend and elder of our church, Bob Cook, who lived nearby. I just wanted to talk to someone who could understand what I was going through. I needed someone who was not asking anything of me. I was sure I could get a grip back into reality. Bob would welcome his beloved pastor and friend. He always had a kind word to share with his pastor.

The dragon within now sensed that I was at my lowest and began to spit its fiery venom into my mind with a new vigor. He realized that if he could keep me dragging as low as I was at this time, he would eventually win. His plan now was to take total control over all my reasoning and strip what little integrity I had left and cast me into some obscure pit where I could swim in the murkiness of self-pity. He must not give up on poisoning my mind and spirit. He had the upper hand, and it was clenching tighter and tighter.

I drove down the dark dusty road of this small farming community. In a distance, I could hear the baying of hounds as they heard the squeaking of the springs of my truck coming closer to their territory. The dogs would rush to meet my truck and bark feverishly as I rode past their domains. Deep ruts presented a challenge to keep the vehicle on the road, which meant I had to maneuver closer to one side of the narrow pass in an effort to miss the deep mud puddles. Low-hanging branches scratched the sides of my truck as I passed the shallow pools of murky water and ice.

As the knurled branches ran their tentacles over the sides of my chariot, I winced as though this pain was against my flesh and not just against the smooth painted fenders and doors. Now my mind sensed that everything was inhospitable when it came to me. I envisioned the Leviathan standing at the side of my path waiting for me to get closer so he could swipe my fleshy tissue as I drove past. My mind only knew torment and now started to hallucinate about figures others couldn't see but were real to me. My adversary was gleeful, as he was winning over the reality of my mind.

As I began to get closer to Bob's house, pride and self-pity began to choke my sense of reasoning. I heard my inner voice convince me by saying, *Why should I burden anyone else with the troubles that I have brought upon myself? I am not worthy to have a friend such as Bob.*

As I drove up to his house, I could see the warmth of a fine family watching TV and enjoying the fireplace at the other end of the room. He was with his family this night, and I know that this is something we should all cherish. He didn't need the likes of this broken-down man sitting in his living room spouting the troubles of the century that had fallen upon my shoulders. It would be better if I just went home to sulk. I slowly drove past his house, and I was not even able bring myself to the point of asking for help from one of the most giving men I knew. My self-depravity had reached the lowest point I had ever known. The dragon rumbled triumphantly as I gripped the steering wheel and steered toward home. He barred me from yet another respite of hope. He won yet another round of my life.

The drive home was only a few miles, but it seemed as though it took an hour to get there. Upon reaching home, I knew there would be questions. There would be questions of my whereabouts for the last several hours. Questions of why I felt that I had to get away from family. Questions about my health as the blotches were getting more severe. There would be questions about the future plans of going to Atlanta the next day. I knew explanations were necessary to calm the fears of a loving wife. I had no answers, no explanations, and no desires to explain. I had no speech left. My heart pounded in its cavity with anticipation of the forthcoming inquisition.

I dragged myself from my truck toward the front door with such heaviness within; it was all I could do to raise my hand to the door and depress the latch that would start the examination of my mind and my motives. I went through the front door and did not even remove my coat and hat but headed straight forward to go upstairs to our bedroom. Donna looked directly at my eyes, but I had no longer the fortitude or backbone to return her looks but instead chose to stare at the floor as I passed her presence without so much as a word or utterance.

She softly asked her first question, and I could see that her eyes were listening intently for any resemblance of the whereabouts of her husband. I could hear the words of her inquiry, but it was as if they were from a foreign tongue that I had never heard before. The voice seemed familiar, but it would not register in my clouded mind. I felt if I did not sit down in a chair soon, the floor would swallow me up and transfer me to a distant place of obscurity. What a relief that would be if I were transported to a place that had no reference points so I never had to worry about where I was or ever dealing with the torments of my mind.

I scaled the steps to the second floor with each foot weighing several hundred pounds. I found myself puffing, as this effort pulled at what little reserve I had left. I found my recliner in the far corner of the bedroom. I looked at this welcome friend and wanted to sink deeply in its deep cotton folds. I dropped my hat to the floor and collapsed into the arms of this quiet refuge. Without removing my coat, I felt as though I could get lost in the soft folds of cloth.

Soon after I landed in the protection of my new haven, Donna entered the room with a look of great concern on her face, as she had never seen this man I became before her very eyes. She gently asked, "What's wrong?" I simply ignored her requests to delve into the depths of my despair.

She repeated her concerns several times before I spoke the fateful words that were unknown to me up to this moment in my life. I softly whispered, "I quit."

Donna's mind now whirled in an attempt to understand where I was headed. In all the years of our marriage and even before, she never heard me utter such a comment as this. "What do you mean?" she asked, perplexed. I had no explanation, as this was new to me also. I had become a man I didn't like but was ready to accept him for what he was. He was quiet and without ambition. He was not expected to do anything for anybody and wanted to stay that way. He was lost and undone. I had become as liquid poured out of the bottle and spilled to the floor, never to be retrieved. My energy had evaporated and was nothing more than an empty vessel where vitality once lived. I was totally washed-out and had nothing further to give. I could never explain that the battle for my sanity was just about over, and the darkness within me was the victor.

I felt the dragon was most joyful at this point. If he could get me to ignore my wife, then he won a major milestone into driving me deeper to his lair. I could feel his hot grip tighten as I settled into my chair. He now wanted me to turn completely inward and shut out all else and concentrate on his needs. Now I became the prisoner of the dragon. He was in control, and I had to take second place to his whims. He stood there looming over me, and I knew that it was useless to refuse his bidding. He was in control of my every thought and deed. Now I only had to wait for the final blow that would end my scant existence.

Chapter 3

The Turmoil Grows

Donna, in her wisdom, called those that were closest to me. First she called my son, Dan Jr., and he relayed all that transpired at his home earlier. He told her how he was looking forward to having his dad come over. He could hear a note of concern in his father's voice and was eager to reach out a hand to one of the strongest men he ever knew. He relayed to his mother that "Dad's voice sounded as though it was distant but recognizable." His hopes were up, as this was the first time his father had asked for his help. Perhaps this was the time the strongman needed someone else.

He began immediately to ready the stage for what he believed would be a memorial event to help the one that had helped him so many times in the past. He thought that Dad had called from home, which was about an hour's drive from his campus, so he had plenty of time to get things ready for my visit. He was out getting pizza, anticipating what he would say to a man that was always there for him.

Now this would be his time to reach his father with a helping hand for a loved one who was hurting. This was the first time Dad ever admitted that he needed help from someone else. The bewilderment he felt as he returned home only to find a note on the door was just another time I let him down. The wonder and confusion overtook his reasoning and felt that, once again, his father was too busy to keep an appointment and something else was more important, so he obviously postponed the meeting just as he had done so many times before. Dad was true to form in putting him last on his busy schedule and dashing off to another demand that was more important than meeting with his son.

Donna then called my assistant, Chris, from work to ask what went on at the office that may have affected my mental depression. Chris relayed that "This was by far one of the most taxing days we have ever encountered in the eight years we've worked together. Anything that could go wrong went wrong. Dan's boss was excessively demanding upon the skills of his main manager. Reports had to be completed before Dan would head out to Atlanta the next day." He stated that he could see the fires in my life slowly ebb, and he became extremely concerned.

Chris remarked that with each phone call, I seemed to shrink further into obscurity and unresponsiveness. It was our daily routine to take a brief walk during our lunch time to get away and pray. Today I made some excuse and said there was just not enough time today. Chris asked if there was something troubling me. He knew that I never lied to him, but this time I commented that there was nothing wrong and I would deal with the demands of the job and the pressures of life after I returned from my brief trip. Chris could only watch as I avoided truthfully answering his questions of concern.

Chris could see by the blotches that began to appear on my face that something was draining the very strength from my life. I was changing and becoming someone he never saw before. He prayed a prayer for his mentor and asked God to intervene in the life of the guy who never ceased to pray for others. I was a man who held the friendship of Chris as one of the highest rewards of my life. Now even Chris knew that I was about at the end of my endurance. Chris related that it seemed that something was taking over the very life of his close friend. He could understand what could possibly sap the energy from someone who seemed to have enough strength for two people. He could almost see the face of the dragon show itself through his best friend. "Donna, I felt so useless in helping the man I have come to love as a brother. What can I do to help the man of God that I know so well?"

Donna accepted this information and description of the state of affairs at work. Now she related to Chris of what state I was in upstairs. He offered to come over and be with her at this time. She stated that prayer had pulled me through many times in the past, and now his best efforts should be in this area while at his home. He was known as a mighty prayer warrior on behalf of others. Chris said that he would have his entire family pray for the man who prayed many times for them. Now he would intercede for the servant of God in a mighty way.

Her next call was to Bob Cook, one of the elders at our church. She gave him the brief synopsis of the affairs that were transpiring with her husband. Bob had no inclination as to how close I came to rapping on his door this same evening. But the monster within me kept me from tapping in to this valuable source of friendship. Now he could hardly believe his ears that Pastor Dan needed the help of anyone. His pastor was always ready to help someone else. Bob determined in his heart whatever this man of God needed he would be there for his pastor and friend. He commented that he would be right over with Judi, his wife. Upon arriving, they huddled together downstairs where I could hear faint murmuring of voices but was unable to distinguish the subject matter. Nor did I care what or why they were using hushed tones.

Bob slowly made his way upstairs to our bedroom to witness his pastor sitting in a chair with his jacket still on staring blankly into obscurity. There was no longer any life in the eyes that made others smile.

"How ya doin', guy?" he gently whispered. No answer. "Work must be really getting to ya lately." Still no response. "Sometimes we all go through a time when we doubt if God still hears us when we call out to Him. I have been where you are now. Allow me to pray with you for your needs."

I sensed the pity as it began to ooze from this man, and I began to feed on it. Yet some small part of me revolted as I felt this unfamiliar syrup being poured over my being. It was uncomfortable for me to accept feelings of concern from someone else. This meant that I was fallible and needed someone else. I didn't like that position.

At this time, an ember of life came into my being. "Please understand, Bob, I don't feel that God, in any way, has let me down. He has always been my solace and fortitude. Today I simply quit. That's all," I uttered. "I decided to walk alone today. God can never use a man that has been broken as badly as I am."

"What do you mean, Pastor Dan?"

"I quit. I give up. Let someone else dance to the tune. My time to rest is at hand. My arms are weary. The battle has been going on too long. I need to unplug from life and just be. I have no more to give to anyone. It's time for me to give up."

"Dan, I am not sure of what you're saying, but God knows your need. Let's just pray and ask God to intervene."

I didn't care what Bob had to say. I felt as though there were no more prayers in my lifeless body. He could do all the work from this point on. I just wanted to do nothing. I wanted to slip into obscurity and away from reality.

His prayer started out asking for the Lord to reach down from the heavens and pull me up to the plateau where I once came from. The more Bob prayed, the more strength I received to utter my own prayer for Bob's family, Bob's needs, and to strengthen his endeavors. My mind felt such great conflict, as I didn't want to be included in praying my innermost thoughts and certainly not for anyone else. Upon completing our prayer, he asked if I would consider going on to the Promise Keepers Pastor Conference in Atlanta the following day. At first I declined, as I had no desire to be spiritual, nor did I want to associate with anyone ever again. His insistence made me state that I would give it further consideration and make my final decision tomorrow morning.

A gentle pat on my knee let me know he had done all he could, and he would have to leave it to a higher power if I was to ever return from my personal nightmare. He quietly went downstairs where the murmuring continued for quite some time.

Then my son, Dan, came quietly up the stairs and over to my chair. He knelt on the floor to my right and spoke gently as one may speak to an older gentleman waking up from a nap. "Dad, Mom's really worried. What's going on? I was really looking forward to our visit tonight. What was it you wanted tonight when you stopped by my house?"

Even looking into the face of my own son, I could barely utter a word of explanation. "Son, I quit. I give up. I no longer want anything from anybody. I just want to give up."

These words were quite a revelation to the young man that never saw his father give up on anything, let alone utter such words that he forbade his son to utter. I watched as his eyes searched the unfamiliar face of his father. This surely could not be the same man that forbade him ever to give up, never speaking of allowing life to overwhelm you. Life was made to conquer with zest and zeal as though it was a game to be played. Now his father dared renege on the very life lessons he lived by for so long. I could see the puzzled look on Dan's face as he did his best to understand why his dad mumbled these unfamiliar words.

"Dad, it's not like you to give up. I never saw you in this light before. In some ways, I find it good to see you are human. All my life, I felt you were perfect. You put yourself through college, married at a young age, was successful in business, and was successful in the sight of the church. That's a tough act to follow growing up in your shadow. I have watched you set a high goal and then achieve what others thought was impossible." There was a certain quiver in his voice, as he was alarmed that his hero was speaking like a man that was about to voluntarily end his own life.

"Dan, I'm not perfect. My faults are numerous, but the greatest success of my life was raising a son as fine as you. You are all my dreams rolled into one. Your success as a father and husband is not based on my efforts, but your own. Please forgive me if I have made life more difficult than what it should be, as it was not my intention. I simply wanted to express my love for the best son a father could ever ask for. My battle is almost over now, son. Learn from my mistakes. I thought I was invincible, but I have learned that there is something inside that can bring you to your knees. The time for me to bow to defeat is at hand. I can no longer continue as I once did. I simply want to stop and give in to anonymity."

"I don't understand, Dad. What has brought you to this point?" The words came very difficult for my son to form as he watched the zeal and passion for life drift away from my grasp.

Deep within my mind, I knew that I no longer had the reasoning power to make him understand the great battle within my body was just about over. I could never explain to him or anyone else that inside of every man is a dragon of some sort. This dragon can take many forms, but it always has the same objective: to strip its host of life and bring the man to his knees in submission to his desires and will. His ultimate goal of this unseen demonic creature was to see men take their own lives by various means, but they must die in some fashion.

Sometimes the enemy uses lust of the flesh to drive a man so far in guilt that he no longer can face his wife, then he can no longer face his family. Eventually he can no longer face his own reflection in a mirror. Still in other means, the monster brings drugs or alcohol into the battle. This is where an outside substance is blamed for taking over the good judgment of the highly skilled professional man. But slowly he tightens the grip on reality, and it becomes obscured to the point where the man doesn't make rational decisions any longer and finds his only so-called friend is found at the bottom of a bottle or in the confines of a needle as the nectar is injected into his veins.

My internal enemy used a form of destruction called ego, which had been developing over the years demonstrated by the many accomplishments of my career. This could also be called pride. The greater the accomplishments, the more I allowed my own conceit to take credit that often had very little to do with my individual efforts but were the results of many competent hands at work.

Whenever a man places himself above the desires of his creator, he takes the place of God himself. My dragon now realized he was winning the battle and was arching his back deep within me where no one could see his death grip. He was now able to slash and rip my inner flesh and cause the pains that no one could see or even imagine. He was more than just winning a long-term battle; he was finally taking over my ability to reason. He was so in control, and I had no more fight within me. I had to recognize he was the victor.

I knew my explanations of what was taking place in my being could not be understood by anyone that has not gone through it. "Son, I just need to rest." I felt my son would accept this explanation as the rest of the world would. This allowed me to return to the self-indulgence of pity without further delay. His glance away from my eyes told me that once again I failed to live up to what others thought I should do. I could sense that it was with great effort that Dan remained at his father's side.

The activity downstairs was diminishing as people began to leave. The soft voices were getting quieter. I heard the front door softly close a few times, and then I heard the cars drive away for our home. After a few minutes, Donna quietly came into the bedroom and knelt down beside me. Dan came to my other side and wrapped his arms around me as though he was saying goodbye to a dear friend. He held me close for a long time then whispered, "I'll leave you two alone. Dad, you just need to rest. I love you, Dad." As he walked away, my heart sank even deeper as the tears flowed down my cheeks off onto the jacket I was still wearing. The pain within grew worse as though the invisible noose about my entire body was squeezing what little life I had left.

Then Donna tried to look into my downward face as she searched what step to take next as she watched the broken man sink lower and lower. Then this beautiful woman of God did what I needed the most. She held my hand as she began to pray a prayer that made the heavens open and the angelic host take note of the concerns of a devoted wife of a husband she was not ready to let go of. She petitioned God himself to intervene on behalf of the man I once was. She asked the Lord to raise me up to a level that He would be proud of. This was the level that I had ascended many times before on the behalf of others.

Now it was time for the Lord to retrieve me from the depths that I descended to. My ears burned as she bombarded heaven to bind the powers that were pulling her husband down into the abyss of despair. She put the forces of hell on notice that this battle was just beginning, and she had the power of almighty God on her side. She was not about to see a member of God's family waste away. She was determined to let all of creation know that this was a man of God, and she was not about to let anything stop the Lord's will to be accomplished in my life.

It was as though she could see into the torment and pain that freely flowed through my body and soul. She banished any form of the evil one that was at war with the spirit man within me.

As the prayer ended, tears flowed down her sweet face, and her gentle kisses flowed over my face. It was now very late, and rest would be needed by all if tomorrow was to be the day I traveled to Atlanta. The soft chair was my bed that night. My coat was my blanket. Donna removed my shoes and bade me sweet rest. It was though that she could see her knight in shining armor had a dull coat of armor and was slowly rusting. It was in God's hand as to the outcome of this venturous day.

The dragon lied down and decided to see if I could recover from the fight that lasted as long as this one. He knew that I was at a new depth that would require more strength than I possessed. It was safe for him to let me think that sleep would come this night. He knew that my strength was all but gone, so now he stretched forth his claws and slowly gripped my interior with a fierceness that was steady and defiant, letting me know that he was firmly planted and was not intent on leaving. Tomorrow would be his day to triumph over me as he sapped my remaining strength this long night. His plan was to utterly do away with any thought I may have of surviving this life. Tomorrow he would plant the emotion of ceasing life as I knew it. His final triumph so he could move onto one more person to conquer. Suicide would become more comfortable in my reasoning process. The very thing that abhorred me before was now a possibility. It now was considered an avenue of rest from this torment.

My eyes were heavy and dry from crying. Each time I closed my eyes, I felt such relief from the pain within. I felt that rest was now my only friend. Come, sweet rest, and let me fall into your arms once more. My mind thought, *What would it be like never to wake again?* The dragon had his final hold on my mind now; he could rest and wait to deal the final blow tomorrow.

As I lie there somewhere between sleep and awake, I could sense the prayers of the saints being presented to God on my behalf. It was though my intense warfare was being shifted from me to other forces. The Lord must have realized that my defenses were completely exhausted, and now it's time to intervene on behalf of the man who had enough. The internal dragon had fought a rough fight this day, and he was not going to have a restful night battling the forces of the Lord. As he was dealing with some archangel, I was permitted to close my eyes and rest.

CHAPTER 4

THE TRIP TO ATLANTA

Waking up from a fitful night, my body reminded me that I was still very tired, as rest was not the friend I hoped for. The chair was not as comfortable as I anticipated it would be. I still had my coat wrapped around me and my hat laid on the floor where it dropped. As I began to gain consciousness, my mind wanted to taunt me with thoughts of doubt, despair.

And things I should've done but failed to do. Then I began to reason a trip to Atlanta would be a total waste of time. The tickets were still messed up, and the long layovers were something I dreaded with a passion. The more my mind raced, the more I could feel the effects of not getting any sleep.

The dragon awoke and was ready to continue the battle for my mind. It was though he knew he couldn't let up on eroding my self-confidence and sanity. The arm of the Lord had been amidst a conflict throughout the night on behalf of one of His ministers. The prayers of His faithful servants kept the battle raging throughout the entire evening. Now the dragon was on the defensive, as his every move was to fight off the army of God and, at the same time, take an occasional swipe at my resistance. If he could just keep wearing me down, he would eventually triumph over this so-called man of God.

This country pastor was no match for this mighty demon. He felt confident that this would be his day to defeat me once and for all.

He attacked as soon as I awoke while I was still in the chair. My mind began to spin with thoughts that brought a new sense of urgency with each breath. Those thoughts rushed in with a new sense of vigor and torment. I doubted my abilities as a husband, as a father, as a pastor, and as a defeated man.

My church didn't understand the demands of the position I was trying to fill. My secular job as a manager could never understand the demands of the small church I pastored. It seemed that every person I cared about could never understand the demands of my many task masters that pulled at me with a relentless pursuit of my resources. These demands tore at my very being. Health issues were staring me in the face as the red blotches caused my skin to crawl to the point I wanted to scream. I tried not to scratch the abrasions, but something inside wanted me to claw the very flesh from my bones. My mind would not concentrate on anything more than a few seconds at a time. Concentration was a fleeting memory of my former self. I envisioned myself as the silver sphere of a pinball on its downward quest to reach the bottom of the game. It was though I was getting bounced back and forth from one rubber bumper to the next. The whole time, the score was getting higher against my efforts to stay out of the pit of despair. The lights, the bells, and the buzzers were distractions all around me as I moved through life.

The words of my son still echoed in my ears. Have I made life more difficult for the ones I hold in high regard? Those words echoed through my mind. I never realized how the actions of one person affect others in such a dramatic way. I forced myself to get up and pull off the clothes that I slept in. The hot shower did not have that refreshing feel this morning. Maybe the numbness of my mind began to take over my entire body; this was another disappointment.

As I looked in the mirror to shave, I came to the realization that everything was in black and white. I lost the sense of color and the ability to even smell the aftershave I had used for many years. What else would this day bring? My mind thought of all the many challenges this day would evolve into. Perhaps if the dragon could get me alone from any of the support of family and friends, he could pour on the destructive blow that would end this longtime battle.

As I came downstairs, my wife, Donna, had the coffee poured and asked if I had decided to go to Atlanta. I nodded to the affirmative. She could sense that I still had very little desire to talk. She could see that a good night's rest would not solve the weakness of this illness or diminish the red blotches about my face and neck. It would only come by the hand of the almighty God. I could feel her compassion and concerns from the other side of the room as she did her best to stare at me.

I didn't notice the deep sense of concern and alarm as Donna watched as I shuffled over to the couch and started going through some of the loose papers and unwanted receipts in my billfold. This ritual was something I often did before a trip to ensure that I have only the essential papers that I need so I can find them when I need to in a hurry. This simple act of uncluttering my wallet was not perceived by Donna as a simple gesture to organize, but an act of simplifying my life as though I did not plan on returning to my family once I left this house this day. What Donna saw was a man preparing to shake loose something from his life. She was reminded how her father would go through this same ritual before he left her mother, not wanting to take anything that reminded him of the pain they caused each other over the years. Donna held back her tears and did her utmost to maintain her composure while this episode went on silently. I could feel her eyes scrutinizing every move I made.

Finally I brought my bag of clothes from upstairs and proceeded to tell Donna that I would call her later. She sat quietly on the couch, not uttering any words, only staring dismally into space while waiting for her time to release all the pent-up emotions. I gently kissed the woman the Lord had given me and expressed my love, then quietly went out the front door. As I began to move toward the door, I felt a strong urge to pray over my dear wife. I walked over to the couch and placed my hand upon her head and whispered, "God, give Donna your strength to endure what she must go through today. In Jesus's name, amen!"

Now why had I said these particular words? Was there something the Holy Spirit was trying to tell us both? What was so special about this particular day? I moved closer to the door, and I glanced back to see Donna looking into her own lap, not wanting to see my eyes.

Upon closing the door, I could hear the cries of a woman that had been deeply hurt, and sounds of great remorse seemed to cut through me as I drew closer to my truck. That's when the monster let me know he was still with me. His sense of triumph ripped through my body as though some cat-o'-nine-tails was tearing at my flesh. He wanted me to get away from this haven of rest and the support of my faithful wife. He also knew that he had to start to wear my resistance down early if he was to see me destroyed by the end of this day. As I slowly drove off in my truck, guilt started to rise up in my throat to the point I was starting to choke.

The intensity of his thrashings within now increased to unprecedented size and ferocity, as he knew that my heart was tender and vulnerable. His greatest weapon was doubt, and he knew when to strike it deep into my heart. He slashed with his great talons at my interior with a sense of fierceness that I had not known before. He erected himself upright as to choke my throat with his presence, preventing me from uttering a word and making breathing difficult and laborious.

It was all I could do to bring air through my nose and then release it with great effort. The internal pain had reached a new intensity. My ears were ringing as the sound of Donna's cries sliced through me as a dull knife. My mouth was dry as I tried to swallow, and it felt as though my tongue was struck to the roof of my mouth. Already this day the enemy within me made me conscious that he still remained in control and was setting me up for the kill to come later. He knew that he would still have a few hours of torture for me before he made the final blow that would bring my destruction in losing my mind altogether or the ultimate defeat: suicide.

My mind began to tell me I had no right to leave amidst all this pain and suffering I caused in the last few hours for my family and friends. I had no right to leave the job at one of the busiest times of the year. I had no right to leave my church when so many families needed their pastor. This was selfish of me to think of myself and try to get away to a pastors conference. I wasn't even sure I should relate myself as a pastor. These were men that *demonstrated* the willingness to serve God in the face of anything. I was merely going through the motions of a pastor now. I didn't even know what to expect from this organization called Promise Keepers. For all I knew, this was a denominational get together that I certainly didn't want anything to do with. I couldn't even keep the promises I made to many others, let alone speak new ones.

The first leg of my new journey would start with the drive from southern Missouri to northern Arkansas. I don't even remember the drive to the Fayetteville airport. All I recall is the pain and torment of a man about to die of a self-inflicted destruction of guilt and remorse. I didn't much care if I was late or early to the airport, or if I even made it in time for my flight. I was steeped in my own world once again. The pain within only allowed me to utter the smallest of responses to people's questions that I met on my way to the ticket counter.

I no longer wanted to be talked to or even noticed. I just wanted obscurity from the world around me. The thoughts of my mind were now screams of torture and despair. They came with ferocity as wave after wave of relentless fear and doubt. Not only were they more unyielding, but they were drowning out the world around me. I could not hear what people were saying to me. I had to have the clerks at the check-in desk repeat things to me several times as if they were speaking in a language unfamiliar to me. It was hard for me to understand why others were not aware of the dull screams in the background. The fog that clouded my thinking was affecting my hearing as well as my reasoning.

I then watched my own hand as I handed my ticket to the agent. It was trembling like that of an older person, unsure of his every move. I must have been a sight to watch as I shuffled along the tarmac toward the first plane of the day. I could tell that my shoulders drooped, and my head was down.

The small commuter plane roared to life as I remembered I always placed earplugs in my pocket to wear while flying. I fumbled the plugs into my ears eagerly as if that would stop the clamor of noises I was hearing. This would also be another reason if anyone noticed the earplugs, they would think I couldn't hear them and, therefore, I didn't have to talk. I pulled my wide-brimmed hat down even lower over my brow and pretended to sleep. I could hear the murmurings of those around me but could not make out any of the conversations. It was just as well as I had nothing to give to anyone. I didn't want to associate or trade comments with anyone. I found the roar of the small plane somewhat soothing and melodious. Closing my eyes only intensified the noise of my inner psyche.

After disembarking from the plane in Dallas, I felt the sharp wind across my face as we raced into the airport. In all the years I traveled this route, the line never moved fast enough for me. This day, I didn't care how fast the line moved, or if anyone pushed ahead of me in line. I was beaten down. I was no longer the busy business traveler; I was simply a face in the crowd. I reached obscurity at last. Then came the long wait in the airport seats that were never very comfortable especially when you have a valise full of clothes and heavy coat.

I reasoned for quite some time whether I wanted to get something to eat or not, but somehow I just could not clearly make up my mind. Did I need nourishment? I hadn't eaten for almost two days. Should I wait? Should I just get something light? Then it dawned on me that I wrestled over the simplest things now. I had a hard time deciding if I actually wanted to get something to eat. Why had I become so unpredictable? I disgusted myself with indecision. So I simply sat and watched all the many commuters hurry past me on their way to a new adventure somewhere far away. I turned to my familiar game of guessing about the lives of the people I saw. This was something I did at every airport. Not just watching the way they walked, but studying their faces, their clothes, the way they clutched their luggage, etc.

That guy is on his way to a business meeting. He is clutching his briefcase as though it has his whole world in it. He dare not let anyone see his great presentation before he is fully ready.

That lady is on her way to meet her significant other. She is wearing a skirt that is way too tight for a respectable lady to be meeting her husband. She is trolling the pool of humanity trying to catch a live one.

Those two are new to this country, as they have a bewildered look on their faces as they drag their overstuffed bags and attempt to read the English and foreign language signs over their heads.

I must have watched this circus of humankind for two straight hours without moving anything but my eyes. My mind drifted back to times when I could relate to the business men in sharp suits and briefcases full of hope and dreams of tomorrow. Often I possessed a look of triumph as I traveled home after conquering another foe on the battlefield of business. But now my arms were dropped at my sides, weary from these many battles. My mind did not want to explore the realms of possibilities. I was poured out as water on the floor. I was a causality of war, and I accepted my fate. Little did I know that the Lord was having a transfusion being prepared for me in Atlanta.

This second flight was now ahead of me. The airport was just as busy as ever with men and women darting past to catch their next flight. Once I found my gate, I resigned myself to find a chair as far from the crowd as possible. For a long time, I just watched people and regressed back to my game of trying to guess where they were coming from or what they did for a living. Now I grew weary of the game and just sat there without any thought of any other human being. I was content to simply sit there and hand-feed the monster that was thriving within me. He absolutely loved to dine on self-pity. The more I gave to him, the more he would stop the pain of his scorching breath within my stomach. I was dancing to his tune to grab any relief I could from the inner torment.

As I sat there, I felt strangely remote from all the other passengers. It appeared that everyone had a purpose or at least a direction. I, on the other hand, was aimless. I didn't care what the flight resulted in or who was aboard or even where it landed. It was my time to just watch as others scurried around looking at the arrival and departure boards overhead and then glancing at their tickets.

Then the ticket agent called for boarding of my flight. Looking at my ticket, I realized that I had made another mistake. My seat assignment was as far to the rear of the plane as I have ever sat. My mind thought of the many flights I'd had booked, and I did not like sitting in the rear of the plane. This part of the plane always had the roughest ride and more ups and downs. I always requested a seat closer to the front where it was usually more comfortable and easier to get off without waiting for those in the rear. I felt almost relieved to be sitting in the rear again, as those seats rarely fill up.

I looked ahead to see people getting settled in to their seats as I slowly progressed my way toward the rear where my seat assignment was. Now I didn't care when I got off. The valise I carried was difficult to fit in the overhead compartment, but with a little persuasion, I managed to shove it all the way in and slam the door shut. I plopped down in the aisle seat in the very last row of the aircraft and didn't even bother to unzip my coat or even remove my hat. I just wanted to be left alone. Perhaps I could hide in this obscure place away from all the other passengers.

Just about the time I felt comfortable, I glanced up to see a well-dressed man look in my direction as he made his way down the aisle and glanced toward the window seat next to me. *Oh no*, I sighed, *not a companion in the next seat.*

Sure enough, he made a beeline directly to the seat and was smiling all the way. "It looks like this is my seat here." He stated with a sense of triumph. The stranger placed all his belongings in the overhead and proceeded to excuse himself for bumping into my seat several times. He found a place to stash his belongings overhead and brushed past my legs as he sat down next to me while I stared out the opposite window, hoping there would be no conversation.

His seat was by the window, which meant that I had to at least acknowledge his presence for a brief instant as he passed me. As this nicely dressed man took his seat next to me, I knew he wanted to talk. His first words to me other than the apology were, "Are you on your way to Promise Keepers meeting in Atlanta?" I looked somewhat puzzled, as I had never been asked this question before. He repeated his question the second time as though I was of a foreign dialect. When I answered to the affirmative, his face lit up, and I could see he thought this was his opportunity to talk all the way to Atlanta. This promised to be another long flight, and I could sense the stirring deep within my stomach.

He proceeded to tell me that he was the senior pastor of some Baptist church I never heard of, and his son was a pastor of another Baptist church while his daughter was a lawyer back east someplace. Not to be outdone, the gentleman in the next seat across the aisle chimed in that he also had a son that pastored a Baptist church as well as him. Just then, another man piped up and said that he and the three men he was traveling with were also pastors of Baptist churches from yet another part of the country.

That was all I could take. Not only did I have doubts about being away from home, now I was involved in a mainline denominational meeting that I didn't want anything to do with. I didn't have anything against the Baptist faith; after all, I was licensed by the same denomination many years prior. I just couldn't see myself sitting there amongst highly successful pastors of large churches while I felt like an imposter trying to keep a small church from falling off the face of the map. My church was smaller than most of their choirs. I didn't have the right to sit on the same airplane with most of these men of God. These men dedicated their lives to serving God, while I believed that I was just playacting in a role that I was not well-suited for. The feeling of complete inferiority overwhelmed me to the point I just wanted the floor of the plane to open enough to swallow me up. It was obvious that the inner dragon was spewing his venomous acid again into my thoughts.

The fiend within me was relentless in delivering his tactics of spreading self-doubt and confusion within the confines of my mind. He knew instinctively that today he would put an end to this war that had been raging for years now. I started to feel more uneasy with every word these men spoke around me. The words of accomplishments and blessings were being thrown around me like biscuits at a bakery. I could sense that as each one talked, they would wait their turn to outdo the next pastor in their quest for submission to the Almighty's call.

My mind raced to understand what they were saying and, at the same time, look at my own failures in comparison. The monster grunted a low groan of satisfaction that only I could hear. The murmur was low, and it filled my chest cavity with a resounding shutter.

He was advancing, and we both knew it would not stop until he got his reward. My hands now displayed a slight tremble as the positive words of accomplishments bounced all around the plane. I actually began to convince myself that it would be better if this plane never made it to Atlanta.

Remorse pulled me deeper and deeper as I thought of the mistake I made in this trip. Trapped, I felt there was nothing else I could do but pretend I was asleep as everyone else sang Baptist hymns and had a great time in the Lord. I didn't even have the forethought to pray to the Lord to get me out of his encounter. The flight seemed endless, as it was filled with talk of the great event that lay ahead. With each mention of the Lord's blessing, I felt as though a great hammer was beating me about the shoulders and head.

Finally the plane touched safely down in Atlanta without fanfare, much to my displeasure. Now was my chance to bolt from this group of "together Preachers" and seek my own world once again. This was my created world of solitude where pity was a close friend and a welcomed companion. As I passed through the gangway and into the terminal, I immediately took off for the shuttle service area to get to my hotel. Amongst all the travelers of the airport, once again I faded into just another face among the many. I felt safe in the crowds of people that had no idea the torment within my soul. They became as faceless as I wanted them to see me.

Upon arriving at the hotel, I could see a line that started somewhere down the sidewalk and into the lobby. Many guests were standing in line with bags pulling at their arms as they waited for their turn at registration. I followed suit with the masses. I could hear the familiar greeting, "Are you going to the pastors conference?" I could only hope no one would make eye contact with me and seek to start the same conversation. I pulled my hat further down over my eyes to avoid a confrontation that I felt was inevitable. I was also still conscious of the red blotches that dappled my skin about my neck, so I did my best to hide these brands of searing pain.

As my turn came to finally enter the building, I could begin to hear woes of many a would-be guest. The hotel clerk was attempting to be congenial, but his patience was getting thinner by the minute.

I heard him say to the three people just ahead of me, "I realize that you think Promise Keepers made reservations for you, but we do not have any rooms by that organization. I'm sorry. No, I don't know of any other hotels that have any rooms. This town seems to be booked solid. I'm sorry. Please step aside."

Once again, my hope began to slide deeper into the abyss. The pounding of my heart could be felt in my ears. What if they didn't have my reservation? This would serve me right for thinking that I should even be here. What if the young Pastor Steve called ahead and cancelled the reservation for him, and they gave my room to someone else? I was sure I could smell the sulfurous breath of my inner demon as he rumbled a blast of fear up through my throat. I wasn't sure that I could muster enough strength to even ask for my room. My mind raced to wonder if I could get the next flight back home and not wait in this line only to be disappointed one more time. Perhaps I could just turn around right now and head back to the airport. No one really would blame me if I explained that I had no room, and I could always make up a ton of other excuses why I missed this event. But it was too late. Now it was my turn with the unyielding clerk.

"Yes, sir, may I help you?" he said while looking right through me. I could tell by his glare that he was tired and thought I must be just another inexperienced preacher that did not know how to make a proper reservation. When our eyes finally met, I could see exasperation and pain in the face of the young clerk.

"I believe you have a room for Dan Craig." I tried to sound confident. But I had very little confidence at this stage. I searched his face to see how long it would take him to drive the spike of rejection into my heart.

"Yes, there is a reservation for you, but we have a slight problem Mr. Craig." Bang! There it was, the blow that was surely about to drive me through the floor and out into total darkness. As the fear of rejection rose up within, I sensed another deep rip from the great talons from my enemy within. The dragon roared with a fiendish snarl as though he was now laughing as I almost fell to the ground. The blood was leaving my head, as I could feel a sense of uncertainty rise up. I knew there would be a problem. *After all, I'm not supposed to be here*, I confirmed in my mind.

"What sort of problem?" I inquired, not ready for the answer while trying not to pass out in front of everyone.

"Your room isn't ready yet. You will have to wait for about two hours as we get around to making it up. We will have to make an impression of your credit card so we can hold your room while you wait."

I stood there for quite some time not knowing what to say. I didn't expect this answer; I almost wanted total rejection, but there was a glimmer of hope for a place to rest. Now I would have to stay at least one night before I could leave on an early flight tomorrow. "Can I leave my bag in the room?" I inquired.

"No, we can't permit that, but you can leave it here by our counter and retrieve it later if you wish." Now he no longer even looked in my direction. He was busy typing in my information as though I had been reduced just another bothersome item in his data base.

"That will be fine," I said with a sigh of relief. The valise began to pull at my shoulder, and I was relieved to drop it someplace close rather than carry it about.

The clerk took my card and made the proper entries and nodded to the corner where I was to drop off the bag. He attempted to project his rather high-pitched voice as he looked over my head, "Next please."

As I turned to face the crowd that sensed my triumph, I stood to one side so I could see the looks of anguish in many of their faces. I turned to an elderly Black gentleman who looked very despondent. I approached the gentleman, and words fell out of my mouth, "If you can't find a room tonight, give me a call. I can only sleep in one of the two beds anyway." I slipped him a piece of paper with my new room number and began to walk away, not quite fully understanding where this short bout of compassion came from. My mind pounced on this thought as a cat on an unsuspecting mouse. Why did I just do that? What did I hope to gain from such an offer? I wasn't here to solve other men's problems. I had to worry about my own challenges.

"May the Lord bless you this day, young man. Your generosity will not go unnoticed." He gently spoke to me. It was as if his eyes could see in places that light has not shown for quite some time. He stirred something but couldn't recognize what it was. His words pierced into my innermost being. A kind word from a stranger that did not want anything from me but was truly thankful for my gesture, my mind could barely take these words in. I had to turn quickly away, as my eyes began to fill with tears. I hadn't planned on actually witnessing a kind word from anybody. My mind could not comprehend anything but being kicked and spit on. What was going on inside me? Why had I made such an offer? How long was this roller coaster ride of emotions going to last?

What do I do now that I have to wait for another two hours? I certainly didn't want to sit around a lobby for two more hours. I could call Donna and let her know I was in Atlanta. Looking for a phone, I finally found the bank of hotel telephones that had long lines of frustrated pastors seeking a room to spend their nights at. I could hear the frustration as they spoke to hotel operators all over the city, but to no avail. I surmised that the wait to get to a phone was much longer than what I wanted to spend. What now? I decided to take the shuttle back to the airport where I could catch a train to the downtown area where the Georgia Dome was. I knew there would be several phones available for me to call Donna from there. I felt the best thing I could do was to get to the dome and find some place to sit and wait for this three-day event or nightmare to get over.

Now I was standing back on the curb, waiting for the shuttle to take me to the MARTA station and then onto the dome by train. I detested making all these stops and transfers along with the waiting at each stop for the next connection. But that was Atlanta, and I was still better off than the many men that were still standing there waiting to be told by an uncaring desk clerk that they had no room.

CHAPTER 5

❖

THE EVENT

Leaving the train station and rounding the corner of the platform, I felt the bite of the cold February air hit my face. As I emerged from the station, I could begin to see a great crowd of men standing at the entrance of the dome. I stood there and pondered, *What are all these guys doing here? The event doesn't start for another two hours. Didn't they know this was supposed to be my time by myself?*

The closer I got to the crowd, the larger it became. They were standing twenty wide and at least two hundred deep. I took my place and stood amidst the hundreds of others and began to wait for the doors of the great coliseum to open. Thoughts raced through my head as swiftly as the wind upon my face. What could ever possess a man to stand in the cold wind, waiting for the doors of this mighty coliseum to open?

As I looked around, I could see a patchwork of humanity. Men wearing suits, some wearing leather biker clothes, some dressed in American Indian attire, and others having pierced ears and headbands. Now what have I gotten into? Then came the familiar greeting, "This your first Promise Keepers meeting?" I heard this phrase several times as I got near to the strangers around me. I tried not to engage in any sort of conversation, only muttering, "Yeah," then I advanced through the crowd to see if I could maintain my obscurity. I looked in the other direction to see if there were fewer men at another entrance, but to no avail.

As soon as my traveling was halted by the masses, the greeting could be heard again, "This your first Promise Keepers meeting?" This time, it was by a man who was wearing a hearing aid and was trying to read my lips. I had to look directly into his eyes this time and blurted out, "Yes, it is."

"You'll enjoy it. I have been to two other events and was really blessed by them." He then told me he pastored a church from someplace I never heard of. I certainly didn't want to appear rude, but I knew it was time for me to move forward in the crowd of faces again. I had never been a part of such a massive crowd of only men. This was so different for me. I tried to read the faces of individuals. An older man stood there with his collar rolled up to stop the cold wind from tearing at his neck. You could see that he had spent many harsh winters someplace, as his skin as well weathered and possessed deep lines from the unrelenting sun.

There was another guy who looked to be in his midthirties, and you could tell he was not used to waiting for anything. As the crowd moved the slightest bit, he did his best to move ahead of others as though he was more important than others to wait outside one minute longer than he had to. You could tell he must have had a privileged life, as his clothes were very new and of good quality.

The man standing next to me had on bright blue and white feathers hanging from his headband. His native attire was that of a Navajo Indian. His leather coat proclaimed proudly, "Navajos for Christ." I wondered if he was ready for a celebration and worship or for a battle.

Funny how you never notice a man's shoes until you're in a crowd. This day, I was surrounded by moccasins, fine leather, tennis shoes, sandals, and even army boots.

Then I began to study faces of those around me. There were some that were old, young, weathered, smooth, men of color, and men of noncolor. My mind then saw that everyone seemed to be in anticipation of some great spiritual awakening that I could not understand. Their faces told a story that I wanted to read, but I did not want them to have the opportunity to read my thoughts. I wanted to keep my darkest secrets deep within. My mind did not have time to think of my desires any longer. I was beginning a quest to find whatever these men had in their eyes, as they asked the same question over and over. I now must find the spark that lit up their faces. What was this event all about? How was I going to act when I met the Lord's agent face-to-face? Little did I know that the many prayers of the saints were being answered as I was on this quest.

Finally, the doors opened, and we were permitted inside. We shuffled along in unison as a great heard of cattle headed to the feeding trough. As the lines pushed forward through the turnstiles, men inside were ready with Promise Keeper literature of the upcoming three-day event. They stuffed each hand with tapes, booklets, and cards. The line thinned out once inside, and I could revert back to just another face in the crowd.

While getting myself acclimated with the unfamiliar lay of things, I spotted a table with books of all types. Books are one of my many passions of my life. I felt my heart race as I wandered around the table of unfamiliar pages. It was a place that I could get lost in for hours and hours. I took careful note of the location of this wealth of knowledge and sought to find a seat. I surmised that with this great of a crowd, I didn't want to get stuck in the nosebleed section of this arena, so I headed down to the main floor.

Traveling down the steps, I went directly to the front, where I felt that if anything was going to come off this platform, it would have to get through me first. To my surprise, the first section was filling up faster than I could imagine. For the first time, I felt that maybe this wasn't just a Baptist meeting. They never fill up the front first. I found a lone seat between two men and asked if it would be all right if I took my place here. As they answered to the affirmative, the next question came as no surprise. "This your first Promise Keepers event?" I simply nodded and placed my literature down.

At last I took off my hat and coat; I placed them on the folding chair and decided to find a phone to call Donna. The lines were just as long as they were at the hotel. I could hardly believe that I haven't found a phone in all of Atlanta to call home. I reasoned that perhaps as the event got started, I would come back and make a hasty call to home. Then the tables of books by noted authors caught my eye again. It teased me by having authors that I had heard of and respected their works.

As I approached it, I could see some familiar authors and a few I never heard of. I was beginning to notice more lines at the tables and even more lines at the hat and shirt counters. Everything that Promise Keepers was about was for sale. My very soul was thirsty for the things of God. I could not resist the thought that maybe one of these authors had the answer of the pain that was within me. I got in line for the book table, hoping to fill a need that no one could understand.

The titles began to speak to me, *The Making of a Godly Man*, *Reconciliation*, *Gentle Warrior*, *Seven Promises of a Promise Keeper*, and many other titles that began to seep into my soul and minister to the hurt that plagued me for the past few months. My eyes were darting back and forth as a hungry man at a buffet table. I couldn't decide which ones I wanted the most, so I picked several that enticed my mind. After I made several selections and returned to my seat with my prize collection of works. I was sure that I could find the answer I came for within the confines of one of these great works. Now I just wanted to get back to my room and begin to read the pearls within these pages. The jacket covers spoke so vividly to me that it was as though I could actually hear them. It was evident that my mind was still playing tricks on me.

The two seats on either side of me were now occupied, and I felt the need to at least give a smile and nod of my head to the occupants. The fellow to my right was the first to extend his hand and ask, "Is this your first Promise Keeper meeting?"

"Why, yes, it is," I responded, trying to be more cordial than I had been previously. He seemed to be nice enough, a lot younger than I, and he seemed to be filled with anticipation and enthusiasm. I could have related to this several months ago, but not any longer.

"My name is Steve. I have been to two other events and found them to be a most rewarding time for my ministry. I am the youth pastor of First Baptist Church of Rockdale, New York." He searched my eyes in what I believed was an attempt to recognize his accomplishments as a youth pastor. I didn't know what to say. I stood there as a klutz and said nothing.

Just then, the Atlanta Philharmonic Orchestra came to the stage and began tuning their instruments. A sense of awe came over me that I never experienced before. This strange feeling that everyone left the room but me was now enveloping me. I felt totally alone yet surrounded by the presence of one mightier than myself. The music started and so did my tears. It seemed the music was a voice sweetly bathing me in wave after wave of gentle whispers, soothing the confusion that had been with me for quite some time. The hymns were familiar to me, but this time, it seemed God had allowed his angels to play angelic instruments on my behalf. The music spoke to me above all others in attendance. The sound became as warm oil that bathed the pain and displaced discomfort to the point that my very soul put everything else on hold, while I came to the forefront to be ministered unto.

I stood there with my heart pounding feverishly within my chest. Something was happening within me that I could not understand. I felt a presence unlike nothing I have ever felt before. What was taking over my senses? My mind started to melt. My legs began to sway with the music. My voice was gone, but my mouth moved in unison with the music. The lull of the soothing sound transported me to another realm that I had never experienced. I was actually surrounded by the touch of an angelic host that seemed to sense that I needed to hear from the Lord at this milestone of my life. Life on earth was so distant that I had no idea in what dimension I was drifting but was powerless to resist. I had no other thoughts except to praise God and his infinite mercy on this broken preacher.

In this enraptured state, I had no realization of the dragon that had brought me to my knees just hours before. He was a far distance from this place. His roar and tearing of my flesh were a distant memory that I had no inclination to bring into this realm. Although my arms ached from the weariness of battle, I felt I could have continued to raise them in worship of the Lord of lords for an indefinite period of time. I felt I could let go of my defenses; the battle was no longer important. Now I knew I was standing in the presence of God and watched as He commanded the heavenly host to minister to one more of His soldiers who was battle weary and needed to feel His divine touch. For the first time, I realized that Jesus was more than just my Lord: He was my Savior. He took on the battle for my victory. He gave the heavenly host charge over rejuvenating my soul. I was handing over every ounce of my will and my devotion for His divine touch to rebuild the life that I let slip into the clutches of a dark force that attempted to pull me down.

I felt as Elijah must have felt as ravens brought him food when he needed rest and nourishment. When he was battle weary and no longer wanted to face another trial or confrontations, God heard his faint cry from within, just as he heard the anguish of my soul thousands of years later. The Lord knew I needed his intervention in my life if I was to go on with the holy calling He called on my life. The dragon was about to face God Almighty for the sanity of one of His preachers. The Lord already demonstrated what lengths he would go to save one such as I; after all, He gave his only begotten son for me, which is the highest price he could have paid.

I stood there for quite some time, swaying as the Holy Spirit engulfed me with His hallowed presence. Yes, the Holy Spirit was now my minister, my physician, my comforter, and my friend. He seemed to be stripping away the hurt and pains that had long been my constant companion. He whispered to my soul, allowing me to let go of self and be void of the world. Now was the time to listen to the words of the Great I Am and to shut out the words of man. My mind drifted into a sense of love and belonging to God that I never before experienced. I knew, for the first time, that the Lord had summoned me to Atlanta so He could speak to me when I was totally empty and ready to hear. I was but a vapor in a room drifting about at the will of my Father. My emotions flowed as a gentle stream. I could sense that while my life was flowing out, God was flowing in. He was replacing the weakness I possessed for the serenity only God could offer. The tears flowed so easily that there was a stream down my shirt and a puddle by my shoes.

I have no idea how long I stood there, but I was not about to cut short the encounter with God himself for the sake of keeping in accordance with the program. This was my time to indulge myself in the most profound sense of communion that I ever experienced in my life. I realized then that it was my choice to stand before God and allow him to minister to me or turn aside and envelop self-pity.

"Please, dear God, be merciful to me, a sinner." I stood there as God washed me in a sea of warm soothing oil that flowed through the air with every note from the musicians. The instruments allowed me to sense the presence of angels, as they stood all around me, singing ever so softly in a tone that hushed all other sounds. I sensed their warm breath on my neck and felt their ministering hands lift me to a higher plane of existence. I left the stadium for a place that was unfamiliar but welcoming to me. I stood there with arms outstretched, but soon the music came to a soft silence and the men around me took their seats for the first time. Now the program began to proceed forth as planned.

Reverend Joseph Garlington stood behind the pulpit and spoke about the upcoming events for the next two days. I couldn't make out every word he spoke but knew I was hearing a definite message. I did not have the ability to bend my legs yet, as I just stood there basking in the glory of almighty God. Perhaps I will slip back to reality later; I certainly did not want to hasten this encounter.

Finally I could see the faces of those around me and could hear the words from the stage. The night progressed with many a dynamic speaker expounding the virtues of a Godly man and the making of a Godly pastor while depicting the pressures associated with the greatest calling a man can receive. These Godly icons of faith spoke to a crowd, but I felt that I was the only person that heard these messages of encouragement and direction. I slowly started to comprehend that these men had been through what I was going through. They were sent by the Lord to minister directly to me. My mind began to focus and see more clearly. I was mostly aware of the ministering angels still around me. They spoke ever so softly, but the words from the platform were enhanced by the sound that came from the host as though it was being filtered so it would penetrate to the depth I had reached.

Slowly I became aware that there were other people to my left and to my right. Then I began to regain focus on the fact there were other pastors from all around our great country that had similar needs such as I. These were ordinary men of all walks of life but called of God to serve. I could see clearly that we have become as broken vessels that were drained of the effervescence of our servitude. I could see a look of disillusionment upon the faces of this sea of humanity as they contemplated the calling on our lives.

Some of us wondered if the high cost of discipleship was worth the price we had to pay for serving our Lord and Savior. It seemed that we stood there for an eternity basking in the sound of this Angelic Host, waiting for the healing process to rejuvenate our first love, which was the calling the Lord placed upon our lives. Truly I was the most needful and the most broken. My life was now ready to receive a new direction, a new ministry all for His glory. I heard from heaven, *Be still and watch as the glory of God comes to those He loves.*

I sensed that the dark monster within my being was bound by the hand of Almighty God. He was no longer allowed to torment me with his deep scales tearing at my flesh. God was now in control. The balm of Almighty God now began to sooth the scars and deep cuts within my soul. I was not gleeful that he was subject to my Lord, as his presence was still there but simply abated for the present. I vowed lowly to myself that God would win this battle even if it cost me my life.

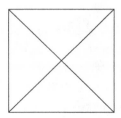

CHAPTER 6

DIVINE INTERVENTION

The program rolled to a slow stop for the first evening. I knew I didn't want it to end, but most everyone else had left the arena. I could feel my self-confidence advance ever so slightly, but at least it was going in the opposite direction from the past several weeks. As I sat there speaking to God, I asked that He be merciful with me and my many faults, and I would try to be more attentive to His desires in my life. We discussed that neither of us ever wanted me to return to the place that I just emerged from. The cost of depression was far dearer than my bank account could afford. If I ever returned there, it may cost me more than I had to ever come back to this place of sweet rest and comfort.

As my head lifted, I could see men busy cleaning the aisles and making it ready for the next morning's start. I rose from my seat and proceeded to get into yet another line to exit the building. As the throng moved slowly through the exits of the building, I heard many times over and over words of acclamation to the night's events and how they couldn't wait for tomorrow to start. The faces that surrounded me were different now. I could see that others had an encounter with our Lord. It was being made evident to me that others had felt the presence of the Lord just as I had.

The line progressed almost as slowly going out as it was coming in. I wanted to remain in the presence of the comforter. My desire was to continue our communion of where this new road would lead me. My mind was far from this sea of humanity that surrounded me at this time. I still had no desire to speak to anyone, but now for a completely different reason. I wanted only to communicate with God. I wanted to be as still and quiet as possible so I may hear His voice once again. If only I could stay in this place of peacefulness.

Then a rather tall fellow to my left looked in my direction and asked, "How did you like the program?"

My mind began to race to speak an audible word that begins to describe the event that just took place over the last several hours. I had not spoken an audible word for almost three hours. My mind raced, as I thought to myself the only words in me were the language that the host had spoken to me in, and I did my best to respond to them in their language. I questioned whether I possessed the ability to make this guy understand that the Lord himself sent angels down from heaven to meet with me personally for the ministering of my needs. My savior considered one as insignificant as I to speak to this very night. Could I ever mouth the words that could relate how this magnificent event, that just moments before, change my very soul? I knew I must try. "It was fine."

We shuffled along a little further when the tall stranger reached out his hand toward me. "My name is Mike Mack, and I'm from Champaign, Illinois."

Looking up, I whispered, "Dan from Missouri." I shook his hand in a perfunctory sort of manner. It seemed awkward for me to look up to this fellow at least eight inches taller than I; he was slightly built and talkative. I, on the other hand, was closer to the ground, and all I wanted was the peace and solitude and to reminisce in the events that gave me relief from the cares that I brought into this great coliseum. I knew the rumblings of the dragon were far from me now, and I did not want the chance to forget that the Lord delivered me this night. It was His hands that held me up from falling deeper into the abyss of obscurity.

Then my mind began to mull over how when you meet someone for the first time, you begin to place them in a category that you want to believe that you have everything figured out, so there is no reason to take this relationship any farther. I wanted to be sociable, but I did not want to leave the presence of God. I wanted to remain quiet but did not want him to think I was rude. After all, I was a child of the Most High God.

"I'm the associate pastor for Word of Life Church near Champagne, Illinois." His eyes were searching to see if there was anyone home behind my eyes.

"I pastor a small church in the southwest corner of Missouri." I had the greatest urge to mention that I was the *senior pastor* but thought better since I was the only pastor, and my total congregation rarely reached over twenty-five on any given Sunday.

"What type of church is it? We are a Pentecostal church." His question started my mind to reel in once again.

Now my mind went into high gear, trying to determine if this fellow wanted to drop names or if he wanted to only associate with like "church buddies." I remembered the feeling I had in coming down here with a bunch of Baptists, and I sure didn't want to go through that again. Then the Holy Spirit nudged my ego out of the way. "It's an Independent Bible Church." Now I waited for the familiar look that said, *One of those, huh?* But he just smiled and continued to walk toward the train station. *Maybe this man is genuine*, I thought. Maybe he didn't hear my response. Maybe he was just waiting for the first break in the line and take his leave of me. Wouldn't that be a switch? At any rate, we both looked straight ahead as the line moved slowly but steadily forward.

As we began to cross over the overpass heading for our train station, the line was still moving quite slow. Mike commented that he was contemplating bringing his car tomorrow for the next event. I chuckled slightly as I glanced over the handrail. "Look down there," as I pointed to the cars standing still below us. "We will probably be back at our hotels before they get on the interstate. Atlanta is known for its slow-moving traffic. You might want to think twice about bringing your car downtown." Mike didn't seem to respond to my summation of the situation below us. In all probability, he must have thought my remarks were heavily exaggerated.

That cinched it: this poor guy has no idea of the traffic in a major city, he was involved in a large church, and he stood head and shoulders over me, so I deduced that we obviously had very little in common. I saw no reason to keep this dialogue going any further. I felt the need to get as far away from him as I could. So I set my sights on moving through the crowd as quickly as I could, and we wouldn't have to try to make conversation any longer.

With my stature, I always found it easy to get lost in a crowd. I saw my chance and made a quick step to the right and then straight ahead for several paces and then another quick dash to the left. I felt confident that a guy of Mike's size could never keep up with my stealth-like moves through a crowd.

As I slowed to a normal pace once again, I felt someone bump into me from behind. As I turned and looked back, I was surprised to see Mike right there grinning a silly grin, as if to say, *It won't be that easy to lose me.* I turned my collar up to keep the cold February wind from biting into my neck any more. It seemed that his night the line to the MARTA train station would never reach the inside terminal. The weather was bitterly cold and windy. I could see my breath as I exhaled a silent prayer in continuing communion with my Lord and Savior.

The men of Promise Keepers are always prone to sing. True to form, the crowd began to sing in unison, "Holy, holy, holy, Lord God Almighty." Mike also chimed in with all the many tenor voices and a hint of baritone mixed in. The sound was pleasant and reminiscent of the event we attended just minutes before in the coliseum. My mind drifted back to my previous conversation with God, and I felt that he wanted to get my attention even further. My mind began to float with the lull of the music.

A strange peace came to me as it had before while inside. I now felt warm tears roll down my cold cheeks and onto my coat. I was no longer ashamed to let others see that the mere thought of God brought me to tears. In fact, I wanted all to know that I considered myself a child of the Most High God, and I felt privileged to know He cared for me. It seemed that we walked for quite some time when the music finally subsided, and then a familiar voice spoke out.

Then I heard the words that I dreaded from a stranger, "Hey, Dan, how 'bout you and I meeting up with one another tomorrow? We can meet at the doorway. Okay?" Mike stared at me, looking for a response.

My mind reasoned that there were at least twelve different doorways into the coliseum. So I thought that if I agreed, maybe that would satisfy his curiosity of this guy I met in the exit line. There would be no logical way for us to see each other amongst forty thousand other hungry men of God pressing to get into this event.

"Sure, we'll meet at the doorway," thinking that would be the end of this conversation. Now I almost felt guilty about misleading him to think that I was actually going to look for him tomorrow. I reconciled in my mind that I didn't want to appear standoffish but merely wanted my space. I deserved to be alone so I could hear what the Spirit said unto the church.

"What time are you planning to get here tomorrow, Dan? The program doesn't start until nine o'clock." It was clear that Mike wanted this conversation to continue. "I'm planning on getting here about 8:30 tomorrow," he stated confidently.

"I plan on getting here about seven thirty. I need to be down front myself." Knowing all the while my plan was to be back in God's house by seven o'clock. I didn't necessarily want to share the beautiful encounter with anyone just yet. I wanted to get back to the Holy of holies by myself. The encounter I had with God made me more determined that this was for me, and I did not care to share anything with anybody. Everything I valued seemed to have been shared with someone. If I could keep this experience to myself while here in Atlanta, maybe I could prolong it until the Lord would reveal to me which direction I needed to go. Little did I know that God might have different plans for my encounter with this rather tall ambassador from God.

"Good, save me a seat if we don't see one another at the door. I won't be arriving until after eight o'clock. Which section will you be at? I'll be down on the left side." Mike had a smile that never seemed to quit. Now he was putting a demand on me that I really didn't want.

"Sure, Mike, I'll see you tomorrow." My mind began to race. There was no possible way that I would ever see this guy again in the midst of forty thousand other average guys. My mind began to think, *If I could just get through this night politely and concentrate on tomorrow.* I felt confident that we would never see each other again after we parted company as casual friends that night. "Sure, see you tomorrow on the left side." In my mind, the conversation was complete.

Suddenly I felt the freedom to lighten up a little, knowing that this encounter was just about over. We approached the MARTA train station amongst a crowd of guys eager to get home or at least back to the warmth of their hotels. The cold was biting right through my jacket, and I had been up for several hours now and hadn't had anything to eat for the past two days; the lack of sleep and food was beginning to take its toll. The line finally thinned at the far end of the train platform. So breaking from the crowd, I walked to the very far end mostly by myself.

True to form, Mike followed my lead to the distant end of the platform. "Why are you down here by yourself? It seems everyone else is waiting over there. Shouldn't we be with them?"

It was made crystal clear to me then that this guy never stood in line for a MARTA train. "The transit system here in Atlanta always puts on extra trains whenever a stadium event takes place. Therefore, the train will be much longer than usual." Just as I finished my sentence, the train pulled into the platform area with the lead car stopping directly in front of us. I watched Mike as he looked at the mass of guys trying to get into the last few cars while our car was virtually empty.

"You really do know your way around Atlanta," Mike remarked.

I sat down with a sense of pride. That's something I hadn't felt in quite a while. My mind began to think how petty it was to feel pride over something as insignificant as a train car assignment. Maybe I was on the road back to recovery. Maybe a blow of destruction was given to the enemy, which allowed me to at least feel somewhat human again. As we looked around inside of the car, I noticed a rather young Black man staring at us with a smile on his face. "Y'all must have been to some kind of church meetin' or sumthin', right?"

Mike was the first to answer his inquiry. "It sure was some kind of meeting. We had the Holy Ghost visit us tonight. I mean, the Lord Himself tended to the needs of many men." I sensed the honesty of Mike as he threw out a line for this young man to follow.

"Y'all need to pray for me," the reply came from this man as I sensed his sincerity.

I wasn't sure of the words that almost fell out of my mouth, "Perhaps you should ask us to pray *with* you and not just for you. You see, if it's important enough for you to want prayer, then you have to start the process with God, and He will honor all our prayers on your behalf." Suddenly I felt like a preacher as I attempted to minister to a man in the middle of a train car on our way uptown.

Mike asked the man his name and said that we would pray together this very night just as the train came to a stop, and the young man smiled at us as he exited out of the car and onto the platform.

Arriving at the airport, it was now time to get a shuttle back to our perspective hotels. I finally would be alone. But my mind began to race as I thought of events earlier that day. I certainly didn't want to trudge all around the metro Atlanta area with my arms full of books. It was now after eleven o'clock at night, and the shuttles usually stop about this time. My constant adversary began to show his ugly face once again. Anxiety crept in slowly. He certainly did not want to miss the fun in watching me worry about a simple thing such as a shuttle schedule. My mind began to play out all the scenarios of what ifs.

What if the shuttles were done for the day? What if there were no more cabs at the airport? What if the hotel doesn't have a room available? What if someone stole my bag? What if I had to spend the night in the train station like the homeless people I have seen on several occasions?

I could feel the mental drain of the day sapping what little energy I had left. I still was a long way from being secure in who I was again.

As we emerged from the train, Mike spoke over the murmur of the crowd. "Hey, Dan, I have to go over there to meet my shuttle.

There are some people I came with standing over there, and I'd like you to meet them. Where do you have to go?"

I pointed in the opposite direction and felt as if I was about to leave a friend I wouldn't see for a long time. I almost felt a twinge of remorse. Maybe it was just more of the many tricks anxiety played on me as he watched as I squirmed as my mind slowly began to bend back to its familiar form. Was this guy, Mike, actually getting to me? Should I make a gesture to exchange phone numbers? Did I even care if I ever saw him again?

"I really need to get near the area where my shuttle is stationed so I don't miss it. I'll see you later." Now I was sure that this was the final remark that I would ever have with this guy. Soon I would be alone and have a time to reflect on all the day's events.

"Dan, let's have a word of prayer before we go our separate ways. I believe God has blessed us this day and brought us together for a reason."

Bang! There it was as big as day! Someone else thought enough about me to want to pray with me. There was no mistaking that to be true. God had taken a pretty rough day in the life of Dan and made it pretty extraordinary. Maybe the Lord had not abandoned me entirely after all. "Sure, let's pray," I mustered. Once again, tears found their way down my solemn cheeks. Someone thought enough of my well-being to request prayer for me. This was just another demonstration of the love that God had for me.

As Mike began to pray, it seemed as if he was a true mind reader. All the questions I had in my mind were voiced before God as a direct intervention for my comfort. I listened intently as Mike made mention of every concern I had for my hotel, my sleep this night, my shuttle being there, and even my family that were waiting for my call back in Missouri. We even prayed about the needs of a young Black man we just met on the train. Mike demonstrated to be a true disciple of our Lord. How blessed I felt to be bathed in his solemn prayer. How blessed I was to be in the presence of this man of God. My mind began to see this encounter with Mike was not just a coincidence or fluke: this was a direct intervention form God to a lonely preacher.

For the first time, I could not utter a word in prayer. This man had said all I felt, and I believed we met the Lord on His terms and the matter was settled. Truly he was being used by the Lord to meet a need I never realized that I needed until that moment.

Anxiety had once more taken a back seat to the warmth I felt in God's presence. I wasn't afraid of the chilling night or the hotel shuttle or even having a room at the inn. I found God in the warmth of a prayer while standing on the shuttle platform with a newfound friend. I came to the realization that friendship doesn't take years to build but relies on the hand of God to put two people together that would never have found each other by any other circumstance.

As Mike closed his prayer on our behalf, a deep guttural groan came from my bosom as if a great release of pressure had just taken place. I looked up to see Mike's smiling face beaming down on mine. His arm was still around my shoulder as though he knew I needed the touch of another human at this time in my life. Then I realized that the guys Mike traveled down to Atlanta with were now all around us. Each one extended a hand to touch the man that Mike was praying for. Each one was dedicated prayer warriors, and if their Pastor Mike felt this man on the platform needed prayer, then they prayed as the Spirit led them.

Looking up, I sensed that these men personally knew the same Lord I encountered this very night. They seemed to sense my needs without knowing anything about me in the natural. After introductions, we said our good nights and went to our separate areas of the platforms to await our shuttles.

My mind was soaring with the events of the day. But now I felt the presence of the Lord standing with me, just as Mike prayed for. I can't wait to tell Donna of the mighty things God sent to enrich my life and bring me back from the brink of destruction.

CHAPTER 7

❖

SHARING THE DREAM

As I entered into the lobby of my hotel, I sensed this was the final leg of this day's journey. My arms were tired, and the rest of my mind and body were not showing just how long I had been without sleep and food. The reception counter was now manned by yet another individual, and yet I now felt more confident than the last time I crossed this threshold. "Yes, Mr. Craig, your room is ready, and there are no messages for you. Would you like some help with your bags?"

"No, I'll manage. I just want to get some sleep. Thanks anyway." I thought it was strange that there were no messages waiting for me. Perhaps Donna lost track of time during this busy day. But she always calls my room when I don't give her a call right after I land in some distant city. Now I trudged along the many corridors, carrying my garment bag; my many purchased books; my hat and coat; and my prize possession, my Bible. It seemed that my mind contained much more than the items that tugged on my arms. My brain could barely contain all the events of the past several hours. My body was electrified with excitement, and yet the weariness of the last two days was also present. Rest for body and mind would come soon and be so very welcome.

Getting in the room was uneventful except for dumping all my things on the floor as soon as I walked through the door. Books sprawled in front of me, and my garment bag didn't make it quite to the first bed before it hit the floor.

While kicking off my shoes, I reached for the phone to call Donna. I knew she would want to hear how the Lord stopped the entire world just to minister to her husband. My fingers tapped in the numbers automatically, because I had done so, so many times before. But with my newfound exhilaration, I thought I would never get all the numbers completed and contain my zeal at the same time.

"Hi, honey, it's me…" These were the only words that came to me as I could hear her slowly whimper a murmured cry. The sound was one of relief. Yet I could sense that she just had a long-awaited prayer answered by the mere sound of my voice. She spoke so very softly. I could barely hear the words that flowed along with her tears on the other end of the phone.

"Honey, I love you. Where are you? Just tell me you are all right." Her muffled voice spoke with a sense of relief at the sound of my familiar voice.

"I'm in Atlanta. I just got to my hotel. Are you all right?"

"I have been waiting for your call all day. I didn't know whether you even made it to the airport when you left. I have called the airline agency and the prayer line for two different ministries when I didn't hear from you. Soon after you left, a man called the house and asked to speak to you. I told him you were on vacation for the rest of the week. He let me know that I was the stupidest person in the world, as he already got that message from your secretary at the office. He insisted that I give him a number where you could be reached, but I gently hung up the phone before he could speak any further."

Now I could clearly see that my inner dragon wanted to thwart my every move, even to antagonize the one I loved so very much. Yes, the demon inside had allies that wanted Donna to struggle with guilt, anxiety, and most of all, fear. He tried to place a seed of doubt and rage in her mind while I was not there to shield her from the onslaught of the evil force that was after me. The Bible states that "the spoiler will come when the strong man is not watching his house." Now I could sense just what that verse meant. The force of the wickedness inside my being wanted Donna to lose her composure and start using any foul language that would drive her deeper into a guilt complex. That was his game to see if he could affect others that would ultimately affect my testimony.

Now my mind moved to Lynsey Ann, our daughter. Over the past seventeen years, we had our challenges raising an autistic daughter. She was apt to have a meltdown for any number of reasons, and many times at the slightest infraction of her world. Lynsey could be smiling and joyful one minute, and then tears would start to flow down her cheeks.

When questioned about why she was crying, you could see her face distort, as the words wouldn't come under her command and she would scream in anguish and frustration. Sometimes the episodes became so physical that I was compelled to hold her arms to keep her from hitting herself. Many times we had to watch her as she unraveled from the natural world and delve into her own world of incomprehensible language and feral eyes. This always was accompanied by loud outbursts and her wanting to hit something.

For the past seventeen years, I never had the opportunity to hold my daughter as other dads did. Lynsey's autism was the type that she could not stand to be held by anyone at any time. As badly as I wanted to hold my little girl, I knew I had to allow God to defeat the world of autism someday, which would allow me the privilege of just holding my daughter. Lynsey was always very susceptible to the emotions of others, so we always tried to keep our emotions in check when we were around her. If everyone around her was happy, Lynsey was the brightest star in the whole galaxy; but when things got too loud, you could sense that the sound brought her great stress.

The world of autism is an elusive venture that many people do not choose deal with. Over the many years in dealing with this condition, we rarely got a break, as some parents do, by leaving their children with the local sitter. We always felt that her unplanned outbursts were something that many people would have no idea how to react to when it came on suddenly. We were never comfortable leaving such a grave responsibility to others when the Lord gave this responsibility to us. Donna and I had no choice, as Lynsey was God's gift to us, and we have been determined to see her flourish to the best of God's ability.

"Honey, I'm more than fine, and I'm back. How is Lynsey? Is she okay with my being gone?" I never knew if Lynsey fully understood that I was no longer in the same town or the same state. When I spoke to her on the phone when I was away, she would always ask the same question, "What ya doin?" As soon as I would say the first few words, she would say goodbye and then hand the phone to her mother and go about her busy day. It always affected me not to speak to my little girl whenever I was out of town. Over the many years of traveling, I became familiar with her one question and then the quick hand off, but it still affects me to this day.

"Lynsey is just fine, and so is Daniel," Donna quietly answered. Daniel was our seven-month-old grandson who I didn't even know was at our house. "They are both in bed for the night. Lynsey has been playing with a Barbie doll, and Daniel has been scooting around the house in his walker. How are you? Please tell me about your day. I just want to hear your voice."

Now my mind could relax a bit, as I could sense that the Lord was looking over my family in my absence. Truly I knew that the Holy Spirit was the great comforter. "Honey, the most amazing thing has taken place here in Atlanta. The Lord himself passed through the crowd of forty thousand pastors to find me and minister to my needs. I have to tell you about a man by the name of Mike Mack from Illinois who actually took the time to pray for my needs. I was truly blessed." After a long pause, I asked, "Are you all right, honey?"

"Just keep talking. I want to hear your voice. I have missed you so much."

"I'm sorry I didn't call earlier. It seems every time I got near a phone, there was a line of at least six guys waiting to get to it. How was your day?"

"I have been so worried about you. When I didn't hear from you by three o'clock this afternoon, I started to panic. You left in such a closed state of mind I wasn't sure if you were still intent in going to Atlanta. I knew your plane was scheduled to land around eleven o'clock this morning, so I expected a call within a few hours. My mind raced to all kinds of conclusions that didn't make any sense."

There is where the dragon was lurking, in the bushes just outside my home, waiting for me to exit so he could plant his seeds of fear in my wife. I could just see Donna feeding the children all the while watching the phone and then the clock. She had a deep sense of longing for one to stop and the other to start. She needed relief.

"After you didn't call for quite some time, I began to worry something terrible may have happened, so I turned to the Lord for guidance. I prayed for your deliverance from whatever changed you from the man I know to the man that left this house today. Then I found a number from a well-known TV prayer line and called it. The person was quite nice but seemed perfunctory in dealing with my prayer needs. I wanted more than this. I wanted someone who could feel the pain that I was going through. The TV was on in the background and I suddenly heard that the prayer lines for the James Robinson Ministries were open, so I dialed their number. I talked to a very sweet lady and I let her know my concerns regarding your state of mind. This precious prayer partner prayed for me first. I could feel the presence of God all around me. Then she got to the heart of the matter, *my husband*. She prayed heaven down over the man I married! Then the Holy Spirit took hold of the prayer, and she prophesied this prayer. 'Lord, not only are you going to take hold of Dan Craig at this Pastors Conference in Atlanta, Georgia, but Lord, have someone there *attach* themselves to Dan. Yes, Lord, that's the word you gave me, *attach*.' Finally I thought, *We have unleashed the hounds of heaven on this man and his surroundings.*

"I waited until 7:00 p.m. before I tried to call your room. I knew that the Promise Keepers conference started at that time, and surely you would have had time to check into your room by then. When the clerk said you hadn't even checked into your room yet, I almost had my own meltdown. My mind raced to all sorts of conclusions about how you may have gotten on the wrong plane, or you may have gotten off the wrong stop before Atlanta. In my mind, you were lost without a trace. Just like my brother Stuart was so many years ago."

I could hear the fear in her voice as she mentioned the name of Stuart, her younger brother who has been missing for many years. He worked in Atlantic City and suddenly didn't show up for dinner one night. They found many of his personal belongings and his car but never a trace of his whereabouts to this day. Donna's mother never gave up trying to locate her son. But a mother must come to the realization that after several years, the chances grow slimmer and slimmer of their return. These thoughts plagued Donna as time dragged by, hour after hour, of no phone call from her beloved husband.

"I then called the airlines to check to see if you even checked in at the ticket counter. They were very reluctant to give me any information. It seemed like I had to tell my concerns to supervisor after supervisor before they let me know that you had in fact gotten off the plane in Atlanta. I thanked them over and over. And now I knew it was a waiting game, but the Lord was on my side. I wasn't alone anymore."

As Donna spoke of the events of her day, I could sense I was loved beyond measure. Not just by my precious wife, but by other ministers who I never even met. Tears flowed easily as Donna told me of the prayer this saintly woman spoke. I listened intently to the hardship I caused my loved ones and felt a sense of relief that my wife turned to God in this critical time. I apologized many times for her pain, but she didn't want to hear of an apology; she only wanted to praise God that He answered her prayers for my safety. I quickly thought of the word *attached* that the prayer warrior used in her prayer, and no matter what I tried to do, I couldn't shake loose from this guy Mike Mack.

I recounted to Donna how I met this man in line when I was about to leave the stadium, and whenever I tried to elude myself from him, he would be there again and again. I told her I tried to dart through the crowd, but he followed me. Then I tried to escape his presence at the MARTA train station, and he was there. Even when we were in prayer, his entire group of guys surrounded me as though I couldn't break free if I wanted to. I finally gave up trying to avoid this guy. It sure was great that the Lord sent a man such as this to "attach" himself to me. The prophetic prayer of the woman who petitioned God was answered through Mike Mack.

The dialogue ensued for over an hour with how I came here with a mindset that was closed and withered. Now I could sense the presence of God unlike I never felt before. I felt alive and vibrant for the first time in many months. I was going to make it. My spirit was now ready to receive a fresh anointing from the hand of God.

I sensed her relief as I went on and on of how the men on the stage spoke words of encouragement to the many pastors filing this great coliseum. I told my wife of the display of a Black minister washing the feet of another Black minister in all humility and a sense of reverence unlike anything I ever saw before. How this great event affected my inner being was beyond my limited vocabulary.

I continued to relate to her how the tall guy by the name of Mike attached himself to me after the event. I also commented that I never expect to see him again but was so blessed that we shared a few brief moments together. I was sorry now that we didn't exchange addresses or phone numbers before we said our goodbyes. In some strange way, I am going to miss not seeing this guy's tall figure and smiling face looking down on me with a set of eyes that knew no boundaries. I could see that his vision was one that reached deep into a person even if they didn't want him looking into their sick soul state.

I must have rambled on for the entire hour; finally my voice became softer, and she sensed it was time to bid me goodnight as the Lord was watching over her fallen hero. He would be all right once again. Now she could sleep the sweet rest of contentment knowing that her prayers were answered by God himself.

We prayed softly and said goodnight with the promise that I would call her tomorrow evening as the time allowed.

CHAPTER 8

ANOTHER DAY OF BLESSING

I awoke before the alarm went off at 6:00 a.m. There was a sense of great expectation in my spirit that day. I felt this day would be even more eventful than yesterday. I didn't feel as sleepy as I thought I would after only four hours of sleep, but I felt rejuvenated as a young minister about to experience a great revival for the first time. I remembered that there was no breakfast served in this hotel at that hour in the morning, so I decided to head off straight to the stadium. I was one of only four people on the first shuttle back to the stadium that day. I surely did not want to miss anything that was supposed to help me climb back to where I truly wanted to be.

I showed my wristband to the entrance attendants as I passed through the gates, and I felt a sense of great anticipation of the events for the day. I knew deep within that God was about to show up and continue to minister to His troubled son this day as He had the previous day. There were new sights and sounds all around me as I entered the coliseum. Yesterday this same place seemed to have no color, but today it was vibrant with the colors of books and the smell of fresh muffins being pulled from the ovens. My stomach reminded me that I have neglected him for long enough.

I decided to look for a seat as close to the front as I had the preceding day before I tended to my nourishment. My anticipation was mounting with every step closer to the stage. My mind was beginning to whirl with thoughts of how the Lord would get my attention and deliver me to new heights that I could barely comprehend. I wanted so much to hear from the Lord this day.

Then I heard a voice call out, "Hey, Dan, over here. I saved you a seat."

I immediately spun around to see the familiar face of Mike smiling down at me as if he knew he would find me among the earliest attendees to this event. My mind raced to establish a logical sequence of how this particular fellow could possibly find me in the sea of forty thousand other average pastors attending this event. My mind began to reflect that he assured me that he was not going to arrive until after eight o'clock, and by then I knew I would be seated and comfortably alone. I was almost certain that I had seen the last of Mike Mack the previous night at the shuttle stop. Now here he was, as big as life, towering over me once again with a smile that there was no denying he wanted to be with me of all the people he could have chosen. My heart melted as I sensed he had a desire to be with me as a newfound friend.

A sense of relief seemed to come over me as if I found a friend that would accept me for where I was at that particular time in my life. I knew that this was a temporary friendship that may only last for the next few hours. I was certain he could not make demands of me as so many others had. I was not his boss, his pastor, or his father. It was just possible that maybe he only wanted to talk to someone as pitiful as I felt. I finally resigned myself to the fact forces greater than I brought this man into my life. Now I was to succumb to his joyful spirit and talkative ways and warm smile.

My thoughts turned to my conversation with Donna the night before about how the sweet lady from James Robinson Ministries prayed that another pastor would attach himself to me. This must be answered prayer. I had a new attachment in my life.

"I hope you don't mind sitting on the inside. I like to sit near the aisle so I can stretch my long legs out." I could tell his face was looking at me for approval.

"Hey, Mike, I never thought I would see you so soon. The inside seat is okay with me. You said you were not going to arrive until after eight o'clock. I got here early so I could go to the bookstore again."

"I really wanted to sleep in, but I felt led to get here early. I am really glad too. This place is filling up faster than I thought. Look at all the pastors here already, and we still have over an hour until the first speaker."

My stomach gurgled to remind me that he was still waiting; I hadn't eaten anything for the past two-and-a-half days. "I'm glad you saved us a couple of seats. Have you had any breakfast yet, Mike?"

"Nah, I just got up early and got myself here. I didn't even wait for the guys that came down with me. Since we got in late last night, they wanted to sleep in a little before getting here. I couldn't sleep, so I just got myself over here as soon as I could."

"Let's go get a cup of coffee and maybe something to eat." I knew why he couldn't sleep. The power of the Holy Spirit had plans for both our lives. He was an instrument of God to help me find my way. I knew that if he did not see me in the first few minutes of this place opening up, we would have never have found each other again. The Lord's hand was still at work this day.

We put our hats and coats on the stadium chairs, and Mike turned to me and asked, "What shall I do with my camera?" He looked around at all the many faces of strangers and reached for my hat, "I'll just leave it under your hat, Dan. If a guy can't trust a group of pastors, who can he trust?"

What a statement. What a demonstration of faith. He revived a sense of emotion in me that I had long ago abandoned. He saw something in his fellow man that escaped the Dan Craig that I had become, a trusting soul. Clearly his camera was very expensive, but his faith far outweighed his concerns. It was certain I could glean much from this pastor.

As we made our way through the incoming crowd, my mind was still amused over how this guy found me of all people in this stadium. By the time we got near the counter where the hot coffee and muffins were being sold, I said, "Hey, Mike, why don't you try and find us some spot to sit and drink our coffee, and I'll stand in line." This was my polite way of saying, *Allow me the privilege of buying your coffee.*

"I'll be over there." As he turned away, I began to analyze the events that led two unlikely guys such as us to find each other in such a place as this. I was trembling with excitement as I pondered how the Lord put us back together for another day.

"Lord, if this is of you, don't let me stand in the way," I murmured under my breath. I wanted to watch how God would use a minister such as Mike to meet my needs. I felt so unworthy to have a man of such wisdom and obvious strength to open his world and share a few moments with me.

Then I noticed I began to say good morning to the fellows in line with me. Then I began to ask where they came from and what type of church they pastored. A smile spread across my face as I realized that I was now one of them. I was a pastor, I was clergy, I was a man that served his fellow man as an ambassador for God. I was attending my first Promise Keepers event and was proud of it. I actually wanted to talk to someone else about the event that was changing my life.

The fellow in the line behind me had an infectious smile that made people want to talk to him. After some small talk, he looked deep into my eyes and stated, "This event is going to change your life like you never knew before. I can see the hand of the Lord about to do a mighty work in you, Pastor Dan."

Now I was certain that I was meant to be here for this time and this place. Could this man actually see what lied in store for me? After reminding myself of Donna's prayer, I knew anything was possible with God.

"Here you go, Mike. I got extra cream and sugar if you want it." I tried not to show that I just met a real prophet of God. But my hand shook a little as I handed the hot coffee and muffin to my newfound friend.

He was leaning against a barrier overlooking the stadium. "Just look at all these hungry men of God waiting to hear a fresh word from God. Doesn't that just thrill you, Dan? I mean, there are all manner of people here, and they came for the same reason: to seek the hand of the Lord in what God has called them to do." We then placed our coffee on the ledge while we devoured our muffins.

Small talk ensued about the events of yesterday and made a few comments about how this event drew out so many varied Christians from all over the nation. Every walk of life was represented here under this roof. All sizes, all denominations and vast backgrounds were anxiously awaiting the next speaker.

"Dan, can I tell you something that I believe the Lord has laid on my heart about you?"

Suddenly I felt my defense mechanisms kick in. I felt as though I was about to be shot for conduct unbecoming a pastor. Then I remembered my brief prayer, "If this be of you, don't let me stand in the way."

"Sure, Mike, please share," I said as if I was confident that anything he could say could never affect me since he hardly knew me.

"Dan, you have a spirit of inferiority about you." His eyes searched mine as if to watch if I would accept this proclamation or reject the word from the Lord and walk away.

Bang! I was shot between the eyes. Mike had no earthly idea of the struggles I had been going through. He could not have any idea of how overbearing I could be in business. He could not have known the doubts I had as a father and husband because I believed they were hidden under all the religious façade I could muster. I stood there searching his face as if it was some great mirror of truth. I put my ego in check. "What exactly are you saying?"

"Dan, you feel that you have to prove your worth to those around you. You're probably a workaholic at the place where you work. You probably feel you're not doing a good enough job as a pastor. You may even doubt whether you're going to stay in the ministry."

The bullet buried deep with my soul, and it burnt as hot as anything anyone ever done or said to me. The dragon didn't want anything to disturb his comfortable hiding place, and this intruder came blazing in with truth and light with a sword blazing. He began to thrash inside my soul and shriek with discontent. He would not allow this warrior of God to take ground back that he had gained. He must thrust out anger and suspicion to thwart off the advances of this trespasser. I could sense anger was waiting just around the corner. My ego was pushing me to reject this observation from a total stranger. Now it was my time to tear his head off and walk away feeling avenged for the words of truth that ripped at my insides.

Wait a minute, could this possibly be the truth? Did I have to hear it from this stranger? Could he actually be a messenger of God sent to tell me how to get my life back in order? Did he possess a gift of the Holy Spirit called *discernment* that I had heard about but never saw demonstrated firsthand?

My anger began to subside, and my spirit began to recall bits of scripture that advised us, "He that has and ear, Let him hear what the Spirit saith unto the Church" (Revelation 3:22). Iron shall sharpen iron, as man shall sharpen man.

My mind now whispered, *Yes, Lord, I will listen.* You will confirm all that this man has said to me. "Mike, you may never know how close you may be to the truth. I will study on these things and pray for the Lord's will to be done regarding this matter. We better get back inside now."

The rest of the events of that day seemed to go past with lightning speed as I watched ministers from all over the country and the world walk down the aisle to dedicate their commitment to God anew. Promise Keeper Bill McCartney was standing behind the podium addressing the pastors from all over our great nation. As men stood to their feet in honor of these men that have been called by God into His holy service, I felt as worthy as any man standing. I realized I never chose to serve God, but I was chosen by a force much mightier than myself. I came to recognize that the Lord had placed me where I needed to be when I need to be there. It was not by accident that I was a pastor of a small country church. It was by divine appointment that I was privileged enough to say I serve God at Bethpage Bible Baptist Church.

Being close to the aisle, I felt the strong urge to walk with these men of God as they marched forward in renewing their commitment of faith. I asked Mike to allow me to pass as I brushed past by him to get into the aisle. I felt the need to allow the Holy Spirit to minister to my needs as I went forward to confess to the Lord that I was refreshed and ready for my next appointment, whatever it may be.

Just as I entered into the aisle, my eyes fixed on the face of a Black man with tears in his eyes. He was a rather tall guy with a kind face, but I sensed a very troubled spirit about him. I felt the strangest compulsion to say something to him.

"Things are going to work themselves out before you get home. Your son will see the wisdom of the decision you made, and he will agree with that decision." My mind raced to appraise what I just said. I didn't know this man or anything about his life or problems. What was I doing? Doubt and fear began to creep over me as though I wanted to find a hole and crawl into it. I wasn't ready to feel the embarrassment and rejection from a total stranger. How would he take such talk from a total stranger?

The man looked deep into my eyes and lunged forward and wrapped his arms around me as he began to sob almost uncontrollably. His hot tears and rough two-day growth of beard was digging into the side of my face. He continued to hold my arms and then looked into my eyes with a grin of acceptance. "You could never have known what those words mean to me. My son and I are attending this event, and I have been praying about this very thing. I am the senior pastor, and I have had to make some unpopular decisions lately. Thank you, my brother, for obeying God. Truly you are a man being used by the Lord."

He went past me now with a new sense of direction and seemed to have a glimmer in his eye that I had not seen before. As I stood there bewildered trying to access what had happened, my eye caught the eye of another man coming toward me. He was a portly built man wearing a yarmulke complete and having long curls running down his sideburns. We stared at each other only for a few seconds when I said, "You are highly favored by God, and your ministry is about to flourish beyond your expectations." I now stood there amazed at my inability not to control what I was saying and when I chose to speak.

"My brother, your words are confirmation of what I feel the Lord has spoken to me, your encouragement means a great deal to me. Thank you for being used by the hand of the Lord."

I stood there amazed that I actually spoke into the lives of other men when I felt I had nothing whatsoever to give to anyone. Then it dawned on me that that is what the Lord was looking for, an empty vessel He could use for His glory with no input from me.

Again and again I spoke to man after man as they made their way past me and down the aisle. Some of these men of God embraced me so hard they seemed to want to squeeze more of the Lord's word forth. Before I knew what was taking place, I found myself all the way down in front amongst men that were now linked arm in arm all around me. Hot tears flowed easy, as I saw faces of pastors, church leaders, fathers, and sons all with a new sense of direction and purpose. I then came to realize that the Lord saw fit to use my feeble abilities to reach men where they were by this most unlikely man. My mind thought back to just a few hours before of how I thought of myself as a man in total failure and of no use to anyone. Now I had experienced two great gifts of God, wisdom and word of knowledge.

I knelt to the floor next to a lone figure and placed my arm around his shoulder. "Would you allow me to pray with you about the need you want to take to the Lord right now?" The tear-filled eyes looked at me and nodded affirmative. "Dear heavenly Father, meet my brother where he is right now, and do not let the cares of this world rob him of whatever he wants to do to serve you. Encourage him, Lord, as he stands before you a broken man waiting for your divine hand to show him the path you would have him to travel. He will give you the praise for what you accomplish with him all the days of his life." My newly found friend let forth great sobs as we both knelt there for an extended length of time.

As the tears flowed down onto the floor, neither of us looked up for quite some time, and then I heard a faint prayer come from this broken man, "Lord, I know you sent this man to help me see that I am worth something to you. I now pledge my undying faith to your service. Forgive me of thoughts of suicide, thoughts of quitting the ministry. I know that this messenger needs your encouragement as much as I. Be with him and continue to work through him. Thank you, Lord."

We embraced each other with tears falling down one another's shoulders for several minutes. Finally we managed to become aware of the many ministers standing all around us with their hands upon our shoulders praying in agreement with our prayers. I lost track of how long I continued to speak with man after man at the base of the stage. But I knew that I was there for a reason. I was being poured out as cool water to this thirsty man that was waiting to hear from the Lord.

Eventually I began to walk back to my seat, and the choir began to sing "Amazing Grace," as I felt that this song was written for my understanding of how I was truly blind to God's provision in my life, but now I could see His hand at work in all I attempted. It must have been a dozen men placing their hands around my shoulder and saying thank you in some way before I actually made it all the way back to where Mike was standing, towering over me with a smile from ear to ear. "You're a mighty man of God, Dan."

These humbling words drove deep into my spirit. I no longer felt the need to dispute the words of this man of God but accepted his assessment of how the Lord used me this day. "Thank you, my brother," is all I could manage to get out.

It seemed crystal clear now why I came to this remarkable event. I was here to minister to those that felt the same way I did just a few short hours before. My mind was trying to wrap itself around the fact that I felt the need to be ministered unto, and I had nothing to give. Now I felt a sense of a new course mapped out for me to follow. I could now look into the mirror at God's man filled with His message. I was to let people know that the Lord has not given up on us, but we have given up on God. I felt invigorated and a sense of purpose that I had never felt before. My mind thought of the familiar account of when Elijah was despondent and doubted the Lord's intervention in his life. But the Lord sent a raven to feed him and gave him an object lesson from the mouth of a scavenger bird.

Yesterday I was like water that was poured out on a hot rock, which soon evaporated. My inner being was used up, and I sensed that I was so depleted that I was no longer any use to anyone. I actually felt that I had nothing to give to others, as I lost fellowship with the Lord. I stood alone and bewildered as to which direction to turn. Now I felt a new vitality as though I was water running down from the cool mountain spring with a sense of effervescence. I now could see that I was to make a difference in the lives of others. The hand of God was upon me. He gave me a new sense of direction and purpose. I was God's messenger once again. I was a preacher of God's Holy Word, and His word was the life water for a dry and thirsty generation of ministers throughout our land. I was commissioned to encourage others as the Lord had encouraged me.

CHAPTER 9

※

THE MINISTER EMERGES

As I awoke in my hotel room on this final day of the conference, I began to reflect on the events over the past two days. I thought back to when I arrived in Atlanta as a broken and worn-out man. A man that made every attempt to rectify all wrongs of my life singlehandedly. I was resolved to give in to the dragon buried within my being who was about to take over my entire life. He was more in control than I was. His strength far exceeded mine, and we both knew it.

The intervention of God's appointed men in my life was changing my awareness of my contribution to this world. The minister and man of God were reawakening and were looking forward each day with a new vigor.

I arrived early at the stadium as usual for this last day. There was Mike looking for me just inside the main entrance. "Hey, Dan, how's it going today?"

"This is going to be a great day, Mike. The Lord has come alive in me, and I can't wait to see what is in store for His children today." In my mind's eye, I envisioned a warrior putting on the armaments of battle and checking his sword for sharpness. Feeling more confident to engage in battle, I went looking for the dragon in the faces of men that I would soon meet. I wanted to take on my adversary if he was bold enough to come face-to-face with God's anointed.

With each step onto the main floor of the coliseum, I felt strength welling up inside me. Clutching my Bible as a man of war would his weapon of choice, I felt strength pulsating up my arm and into my very core. I sensed people saw me differently now than they did two days ago. I was ready to meet any foe that the Lord would have me face. I came to realize it was not by my strength and not by my power but the Spirit of God permeating throughout this great arena. I was no longer alone, but I was embraced by the very arms of the Comforter, the Great I Am. Mike also possessed this aura about him as well.

Mike placed his arm around my shoulder as an older brother would do to his younger sibling and led me down the aisle to a definite place he had in mind. We found two seats in front of the group that Mike had traveled down from Illinois with. It took no time for Mike to guide me over to his group of fellow ministers and present his newfound friend. "Hey, guys, I want you to meet Dan. He is the guy I have been telling you about. He comes from Missouri where he pastors a church."

It seemed like the Illinois team gathered around me as a group of curious birds would a newfound slice of bread and began to introduce themselves. Each one had a short introduction of their place within their church and the Lords' calling for their lives. I wasn't able to remember all their names, but I recall their faces as I watched each one look into my eyes and ask questions such as, "Hello, Dan. I'm John. Have you been enjoying the conference?" a rather slightly built guy asks. "Mike tells me that you have done some preaching in the mission at Atlantic City. I preach in the jails and streets. I find it to one of the most rewarding experiences of my life." I could see the zeal in this man's face as he looked for some recognition in my eyes as to the struggles mission preachers face each day.

"John, I believe the Lord wants each of us to get out of the boat and go where the fish are. I mean, if we stay in the boat, or the church, we don't come in contact with people that need the Lord as much as those still in the water. It's time for us to learn the lesson that the Lord Jesus taught His disciples: 'Go ye into all the land, teaching and baptizing in My name.'

"John, I am no longer unable to just sit and soak in a comfortable church and allow the pastor or minister to do all my thinking for me. I feel you are the same way, John. God has put me on fire, and people want to come and watch me burn. Each born-again disciple of the Lord has been given a talent and direction as a unique gift of God. What we do with it is our gift back to God. You can keep your gifting to yourself and not use what talents the Lord has given you, and I believe the Lord will rescind it and allow someone else the opportunity to use it. You can also choose to use your time, talents, and treasures for the glory of the Lord and to stretch your efforts and then watch how God will fill your cup up again to overflowing with His divine resources. We don't have the option of waiting for opportunity to see people moved into making a decision while visiting our churches. We must take the message to them.

"When people come to our churches, they may hope they hear something from the pulpit that will change their lives for all eternity. We should be a walking sermon for each person to see and hear. This will make more of an impact than a riveting sermon from a pulpit. People want to know how to apply the principles that they hear from ministers. We are their examples, John, so we must lead the way."

John slowly grinned at me and turned to Mike who was standing close by. "We need to have this guy come to our church and let everyone hear him. He is a natural evangelist. More people need to hear what the Lord has laid on his heart. You were right, Mike, he is on fire."

Man after man waited to extend their hand and shake mine with polite conversation of their experience with our Lord and Savior. I seemed to draw an unusual strength from these men that came from Illinois to Atlanta in an effort to know more about God and learn how they could be used for His glory. As each man spoke of how he was changed by the hand of the master, I reflected on my own metamorphosis of the past two days as these guys spoke. I felt a new sense of respect for myself. I felt worthy to be here amongst these pillars of faith. I noticed my head was held high and my eyes keen to the slightest hint of a man that needed a word of encouragement.

My mind began to wonder now, Was it possible that I actually slew the dragon that had laid hold of my inner being? Could it be that I had emerged from the depths of despair to a new plateau of confidence? This was more than I could hope for.

I knew my internal demon was somewhere not far away, lurking and waiting for the right moment to emerge and regain his prominence in my life. It was up to me to be mindful that I needed to think of the wise counsel of the Word of God, "Whatever things are true, whatever things are noble, whatever things are just, whatever things are pure, whatever things are lovely, whatever things are of good report, if there is any virtue and if there is anything praiseworthy, meditate on these things."

This familiar verse now took on a new meaning for me. As I thought about this verse, I came to realize that now my thoughts could aid me in determining what I did with the rest of my life. I could accept defeat from the claws of my enemy, or I could live a victorious life by keeping my eyes on the master of my domain, the Lord Jesus. I was determined to become known as a man that was in the clutches of death, and I emerged to a full life once again. I had been given a second chance on life. I was now God's instrument to be used as He saw fit.

We took our seats once again to hear more anointed men of God speak to the crowd about the life of a minister. Then Bill McCartney and Dale Schafer, founders of the Promise Keepers movement, stood before the assembled crowd and asked for all the ministers both in the audience and on the stage to listen as the Atlanta Covenant was read. A hush fell over the entire assembly as these solemn words were spoken to each man there by Dale Schafer:

> Our great and awesome God, in Your sovereignty, You have brought us as clergy to Atlanta. You have met and dealt with us in powerful ways. You have been faithful with all Your Promises and loving toward us in all ways. We now stand before You broken and humbled, called to Sheppard and pastor Your church, believing that you are

willing and ready to give a fresh outpouring of Your Holy Spirit on Your church. Our eyes are focused on Your only son, Jesus Christ, the perfector and finisher of our faith.

We acknowledge, confess, and repent before you that although we may not be guilty of all that is stated below, we are prompted by godly sorrow to repent because we as clergy have sinned against you (1 Corinthians 7:10–11).

Therefore, we enter into this Atlanta Covenant with You and with each other.

1. We covenant by God's grace to honor Jesus Christ through worship, prayer, and obedience to Your Word through the power of the Holy Spirit.
    *   We have grown cold and distant in our communication with you. We wholeheartedly commit to pursue an ever-deepening relationship with You through worship and prayer. As You lead, we commit to fast and pray for the revival of our own hearts, for our churches, and for the church of Jesus Christ.
    *   Where we have disobeyed you, we commit to be obedient to Your Word regardless of the cost.
    *   Where we have quenched the Holy Spirit, we commit by God's grace to keep in step with Your daily activity and leading.
2. We covenant by God's grace to pursue vital relationships with a few other clergymen, understanding that we need our brothers in ministry to help us keep this covenant.

- We have resisted affirming accountable relationships with other brothers. We commit to pray intentionally for these relationships and seek this support, never again to be a loaner in ministry.

3. We covenant by God's grace to practice spiritual, moral, ethical, and sexual purity.

   - Where we have conformed to the world, we commit to place other gods before you no longer, the one true God.

   - Where we have excused our moral and sexual sin and been neither repentant nor broken, we now offer our bodies to You as living sacrifices and ask that You transform our minds and hearts by Your Word and Your Spirit.

4. We covenant by God's grace to build strong marriages and families through love, protection, and biblical values.

   - Where we have neglected our home fronts as the first place of ministry, we covenant to recapture the hearts of our wives and children by giving them first priority in our prayers and schedules.

5. We covenant by God's grace to Your calling to pastor Your people and to lead Your church faithfully in fulfilling Your mission.

   - Where we have neglected our call, we wholeheartedly recommit ourselves to the ministry of prayer and the study of Your Word.

   - Where we have driven our people rather than led them, acting as if being a pastor was simply a job and not a holy calling, we commit and pray ardently and regularly with love for our flock, recognizing that You have called and placed us in the church that we serve.

- We have used our ministry as a platform for our personal gain, we repent and recommit ourselves to serving Your kingdom and the growth of your people.

- Where we have trusted ourselves and the programs of men rather than seeking You and Your way, we commit to seek Your heart and direction for our churches.

- Where we have lost confidence and passion in our preaching, we commit to feed Your people with Your Word faithfully and passionately.

6. We covenant by God's grace to reach beyond any racial and denominational barriers to demonstrate the power of biblical unity.

- Where we have ignored praying and working with fellow pastors of different denominations and race, we commit to seek out clergy of differing denominations and races, intentionally pursuing relationships with them, praying, and working together for the building of the kingdom of God.

- Where we who are Anglo have enjoyed the advantages that have come to us as a result of the teaching of White superiority against people of color, we confess this as sin. With Ezra, Nehemiah, and Daniel, we confess the sins of our forefathers who disobeyed Your Word and at times stole, killed, enslaved, broke treaties, demeaned, and lied to people of color. Where we have done little to confront the sin of racism in our churches and to halt the erosion of trust between our largely Anglo churches and the churches of color, we now acknowledge and confess that this is sin against You and repent of our sin, trusting that it will lead us to reconciliation and restoration with our brothers in Christ. We now want to do justice, love, kindness, and to walk humbly before You, and we commit to learn so that we might teach and lead our people in the area of racial reconciliation.

7. We covenant by God's grace to influence our world, being obedient to the Great Commission and the Great Commandment.

- Where Your church has lost its saltiness and the light in our nation, we covenant to lead Your people to seek God's face for the healing of our land.
- Where we have lost Your vision to reach all people groups with Your amazing saving grace, we covenant to give to others freely what You have given to us.
- Where we have strayed from the Gospel of Christ, we covenant to preach with renewed passion and conviction the Gospel of Jesus Christ.

In total devotion to Christ as the Chief Shepherd of the Church, we commit ourselves to these things by the power of the Holy Spirit.

> To that end, we give our lives as clergy to pray, to prepare, and to minister for nothing less than a spiritual revival in Your Church that Your body might increasingly become a bride without spot or wrinkle. "We pray that together we might be brought to complete unity in You so that the world may know that You sent Your son Jesus Christ, and that You love them as You loved us" (John 17:20–23). To this we pledge ourselves.

As these words were read over each minister, there I felt that they were directed directly at me and me alone. This declaration was something that clicked inside me. This was a banner I wanted to be under. With each sentence of this sacred document, I envisioned a warring angel of the Lord look straight into the eyes of the Leviathan within me and take back those things that were stolen from my inner soul. I envisioned this warrior of God drawing his sword high into the air and strike blow after blow into the scaly form of my inner dragon. Each sentence drew more wounds on the adversary.

When Dale Schafer read the sentence about "We have grown cold and distant in our communication with you," the dragon raised his head high as if to say this is my favorite blow against this man of God. It was true that my fellowship with the Lord and Master of my life had grown cold and distant. I gave over the power to feel the presence of the Lord to my inner self-pity. The strength of this area of my life was now possessed by the evil one who gained strength from my weakness. It was as though I felt warm and safe under the wing of my personal dragon.

As I stood there watching the glaring eyes of the dragon and the unwavering strength of the angel of God, my mind raced as to who would prevail. As tears ran down my face and onto the tops of my shoes, my head slowly rose toward heaven, and a soft voice came from my throat, "Lord, forgive me, for I have sinned against you and you alone. Help me, Lord, to be more of a man that you can use for your glory. Allow me to decrease so that you may increase. I will worship you from this day forward without any reservation. Return unto me the joy of Your salvation." I felt the blow of the mighty sword slash the flesh of the dragon and his scales fell to the ground. This was what the Lord had been waiting for, to allow Him to be pre-eminent in my life.

Try as the dragon might, he was no match for the power being unleashed by God himself on my behalf. Each point the speaker made drew a new fierceness of this enemy within. He was now fighting for *his* life. His bloodcurdling screams reached a fierce pitch as his scales felt the sharpness of the angel's sword as it came down with the vengeance of Almighty God. He was losing the grip of fear and doubt and had to watch as it was being replaced with confidence and purpose. I could feel the battle as it raged within me. The talons of the mighty dragon began to loosen their grip on my throat, and I felt that I could breathe a sense of clean air as it rushed into my lungs. I felt as though I could sing a new song of freedom and salvation from a torturous death.

As I looked around the stadium, I could see the many seats filled with men of God seeking the presence of the Lord in their own lives. I sensed a feeling that the Lord had sent these ministers to Atlanta to retrieve one of His own. The loneliness and insecurity I once possessed were gone. Now I stood proudly as tears flowed down my cheeks and onto the floor as a Champion of the most high God. I was a conqueror of my inner domain. I was now ready to complete my final transformation. I wanted to get back to the world that I had left. I wanted to go home and conquer my fears. I was equipped to face whatever battle I had to as I was no longer alone. The hand of God was upon me once more. This time he was sending a warrior back into battle with new armament and a new battle cry. I was to take no prisoners in this battle.

CHAPTER 10

THE HOMECOMING

The flight home was going to be quite different than the flight down to Atlanta. As I stood in the ticket line in front of the counter for my airline, I looked on faces now and could see the very souls of men and not just an outline of a man. Now I recognized the many different prominent pastors of the area I was from. They were busy on the phone or reading the newspaper. They were returning to life that they had left three days ago and were ready to pick back up right where they left off.

I could not ration in my mind that they ever attended the same event that I just came from. I could not comprehend why they did not feel the same way I did. Didn't they know that my life was radically changed and everyone should be able to see that I had a personal encounter with the third person of the godhead? Surely I must be radiating a heavenly glow as Moses did when he came down from Mount Sinai. God Himself revealed His divine impartation directly into my life. I searched their eyes to see if they could now see the presence of the Lord in a man that, just a few days ago, was dead for all purposes and now was full of life. My zeal abounded within me to the point that I wanted to shout and sing all over the airport.

As I handed my ticket to the young lady behind the ticket counter, I smiled and looked directly into her eyes. "Good morning,

Mr. Craig, going to Fayetteville today?" the young lady asked very professionally.

I nodded in agreement and said, "I am going home to my family. I have had a great time here in Atlanta, but now I want to see my girls." I knew I must have looked quite amusing, as the smile was large as life itself and the gleam in my eyes radiated all over my countenance. But I did not feel the least bit uncomfortable with my new found wardrobe of contentment and absolute peace. In my mind, I thought that people should be able to barely look at the now bright armor of a warrior for the cause of Christ.

Now this young lady looked more at me and not just through me. "You change planes in Dallas and then onto Fayetteville. There may be a chance of snow, but no delays are shown. Have a nice flight and nice day." Now I could see that my smile was contagious. She was washed in a radiance that I had not seen before. Her smile was warm and friendly, and she looked as though she was waiting for a kind word from someone in her many dealing with people all day.

"Not only am I going to have a great day, but I feel the rest of my life is going to absolutely wonderful." The lilt in my voice seemed to transcend the counter and into her very being as she now smiled a wide grin and sparkle in her eye. Truly the light of the Lord can spread from one human to another with just a nice smile and gentle word.

I took my boarding pass and turned to look at all the many awaiting passengers traveling all over God's creation. As I sat in one of the many seats, I watched as people went about their daily lives as though they all the time in the world to make a difference in God's allotted time here on earth. My mind wandered as I watched these many people looking at their watches, tugging at their luggage, or murmuring to their traveling companion. I wondered what their relationship with God was as they went about their hurried lives. Was this how it was going to be from now on?

Will I only be concerned with the state of men's souls even before I meet them? The Lord was still building me into what He wanted me to be for His glory. The Holy Spirit allowed me to know that He was still with me even now.

The past few days allowed me to see the presence of the Lord on many different faces all over that stadium. My mind raced back to the men that wept openly as I spoke to them through the unction of the Holy Spirit. I remembered the tears that flowed down the cheeks of these men and of my own face as we embraced and bonded as men of different backgrounds yet the same Lord, men of different color but the same Spirit, men with varying needs but the same God.

Then I came to the realization that not all men saw the same things that I saw while standing in that great coliseum. We were men from all over the country with different backgrounds, different church affiliations, and many different beliefs.

My mind thought back to the Book of Acts in the Bible where the author, Luke, describes Paul's encounter with the Lord while on the road to Damascus. Paul was on a journey to do what he believed was the right thing to do. He was known as a man with a mission to persecute the disciples of the Lord at all costs. He could only see what he wanted to see. He was totally consumed with his own desire and nothing else. He had a reputation as a man that will get the job done for his leader.

While on his journey to Damascus, Paul was stopped by a brilliant light that shone around him from heaven. It was at this time that Paul heard a voice from heaven, asking him why he chose to persecute the Lord Himself. The men that were with him during this event stood speechless while they could hear the conversation between Paul and the Lord but could not see any human from round about.

The same voice that gave Paul instructions spoke to me in Atlanta. Paul the Apostle was blinded by the hand of God, so he had to be totally dependent on the Lord to lead him to a street called Strait. He had to wait until the Lord brought forth another man that would lead him by the hand to a place where he could get full restitution of his sight. Now it was clear that I still had many steps to fulfill the will of the Father in my own life. The mighty hand of God led me from a place of obscurity to a place where I found new life.

For the first time in many months, I could see clearly the world around me was full of opportunities to serve others and not be a slave to any man. I would be a man of integrity and not just another guy scratching his way through life by any means possible. I set my face toward the Lord and would never look back. He would be my shield, my guide, and my comforter. I would never be alone again; I had the joy of the Lord deep in my being.

I was privileged to attend a pilgrimage that resulted in the most dramatic religious experience of my life, while others merely attended another conference their church sent them to. My encounter was fashioned by the very hand of God, orchestrated by the Holy Spirit. I was a changed man and vowed never to return to the dark abyss I have traveled from. I had a sense of direction and a purpose that others may never fully understand.

I was more anxious than ever to get home and relate the many facets of these past few days with those that I loved and knew that they would see a change from the man they knew a few days ago. My mind raced to think of what Donna would see as she looked into the eyes of a man that she thought she would never see again. How would she react to my newfound commitment to our Lord and Savior? Would I ever be able to relate to another human being what I encountered as a man that was on the brink of a total meltdown? My heart raced with great anticipation of the next few hours of traveling home. The plane ride was just as eventful as the trip down. Now it seemed that others were quiet, and I wanted to be the one to share of the great experience of attending an event that changed my way of looking at people.

The plane was now filled with every walk of humanity and not just pastors on their way to a conference. This was everyday life on an airplane. Babies were crying, mothers were waiting on children, men were trying to sleep as people waited anxiously as the beverage carts were pulled from one end to the other.

As I sat quietly in my seat reading my Bible, I noticed the gentleman next to me looked out the window, trying not to engage me in conversation. I could really relate to this man as it seemed, but a few hours before, I did not want to say or talk to anyone closer to God than I was. Now I felt that I was in the possession of a whole tray full of diamonds, and I wanted to give them to anyone who wanted them. But they could not see a host of great wealth, merely a guy and a Bible.

"Where you headed to?" I asked.

"Dallas is home for me. What about you?"

"Dallas and then onto Fayetteville, Arkansas then home to Missouri."

He looked away again to tell me that the conversation was over. I returned to my Bible and came to the realization that not everyone wanted to engage in conversation about any subject, let alone the Bible. What a pity that I was sitting here with such a great wealth of riches free for the taking, and this poor soul did not even want to take a peek at what I had. My heart sank as I sat there wanting to share and not seeing the slightest hint that this man wanted to hear what I had to say.

I closed my eyes, and my mind drifted to the words I would use to share with Donna about the life-changing events I had encountered over the past three days. How could I verbalize the sense of freedom I now felt? Just a few short days ago, my world was ready to crash in on me crushing me into obscurity. Now I felt as though I could fly above the clouds, above any problem. I was almost invincible.

I settled back into my seat waiting for the face that would greet me as a new man of God, a champion of men with a mission from the hand of the Almighty.

My plane landed at Fayetteville with a slight dusting of snow covering the runway. Now there were no thoughts of anything going wrong, for I was God's anointed and nothing would happen to me before my time. God had supercharged me for a new venture, and the weather would be at His command.

My truck had the cold white film of new snow on the hood, but it didn't deter me from heading straight home; for I wanted to see the face of the prayer warrior who brought me back to reality.

As I pulled into the driveway of my home, my heart pounded as though I was about to meet someone of high importance that I never met before. I could feel my pulse race as I got closer to the front door and thought of so many things that I rehearsed to say. With luggage and books in both hands, I went through the door and spotted Donna sitting in the chair in the living room. I gently laid down all my parcels and went directly over to the chair and watched Donna's eyes watch me. Her eyes were full of anticipation and hope. Yet they also reflected relief and contentment that I was home once again. This was the moment that I had anticipated for the past several hours.

I leaned over and kissed her gently for what seemed like a very prolonged time. As she looked into my eyes once again, she began to speak, and I held up my finger to her lips and said, "Allow me to first apologize for not being a very good husband to a woman who deserved much better."

She began to speak again, "You're a good husband, Dan." Her eyes searched mine in bewilderment.

Once again, I placed my finger to her lips and said, "I know in my heart that I should have been a better husband than the one I have been. Now I am asking for your forgiveness for all the mistakes I have made during our life together. You stood with me through many tough times and encouraged me to continue. I overlooked your hard work, your dedication to me and our children. You have made our house a home of care and peace. I have done all I could to tear this peace from its frame and stood back and watched as you sewed it back together with loving hands that seemed to be tireless.

"My mind recalls the many times we placed my career and my aspirations ahead of this family. You stood and attempted to warn me when I began to get off track, and I never thanked you for the good that was in me fashioned by your efforts. Never again will I take those things for granted. Now I vow to you that if you will forgive me, I will work the rest of my life to demonstrate the undying love that I have for the woman that God himself gave to me as my helpmate. I now realize that God has had a divine hand in our marriage all along. It took me going to Atlanta to find the greatest treasure I could ever hope to enjoy, right here in my own home in the arms of the one I love so very much. The Lord has transformed me into a better man. I am not perfect, but I am dedicated to improve our quality of life together. I need to start with my devotion to our Lord and also my devotion to you."

Donna looked deep into my eyes and said, "If the Lord has laid the need for you to ask forgiveness of me, then you have my forgiveness. I vow to accept the man that the Lord has made over these past few days, and I will watch as He molds you into the man of God that he wants you to be."

With tears in both our eyes, we held each other as I traced her scent as her hair brushed past my nose. I always loved the scent of my wife. It made me realize that I was home and safe. This was a place where I was loved for what I was.

Soon after my arrival home, I told Donna that I now needed to ask forgiveness of my church. I was not the pastor that this flock needed to lead them to the green pastures that they deserve. This Sunday, I will officially tender my resignation of the church that has come to mean so very much in my life. I felt, this way, they would be free to fill this position with a man of God that had a new vision and would take them to a higher plane than what I have done for the past five years. This decision was one that did not come easily, but I would pray that the will of the Lord be done in all matters of my life. I did not want to stand in the way of the Lord in any area of my life. I knew in my heart that my efforts to pull this small church together for the glory of God was lacking, and I was standing in the way of something better.

Sunday rolled around, and I rehearsed what I would say to this group of people that watched me become a better pastor due to their efforts. My mind thought of how I would give them the option of opening this pulpit to a different man if that were the will of this congregation. I thought of the many sermons that this congregation has heard come from me.

Sometimes I was a real ball of fire that preached as though the Lord Himself was standing there, pushing me onto a powerful message. The times of great fun also danced through my memory as well. Like the time we had during the middle of my sermon when a stray cow got out of the fenced pasture and stood under the window next to the front of the church and bellowed in time with my delivery of my main point. Then there was the time as I stood behind the pulpit facing the congregation when a stray groundhog peered in the open door of our church looked around and waddled down the steps onto the front lawn. I could never explain to the rest of the church what I just saw but I completely lost all resemblance of order of thought.

Now I must put words together to let these fine folks know that there was a need for a change. No matter how many times I rehearsed the words in my mind, I was certain they would not come out in the correct order.

As usual, we arrived at the church before anyone else, and my mind looked at all the many familiar sights that I came to love; but they now seemed to take on a beauty that I never really noticed before my encounter. Now the streaming broke out front of the church made a gentle babbling and melodious sound that I never noticed even though I baptized my own daughter in this very stream. The wind in the walnut trees sang a familiar melody to my ears as I watched some of the last leaves fall to the ground. These leaves hung on through the cold winter but finally gave up their grasp to allow new leaves to take their place on the branches of these colossal giants. These same guardians watched contentedly as many noble pastors walked into this small country church over dozens of years. Now they seemed to welcome me home after a long sabbatical where I found some secret that allowed me to hear their song in a way I never heard before.

I felt at peace with my decision to allow these dedicated people to search out a new pastor. Each face came to my mind, and I felt warmness for their needs over the years and recounted how they interwove through my life. Truly we needed to hear from heaven if the Lord's will was to be done this day. I knew it was time to speak to God alone for guidance to this most difficult decision.

"Oh, Holy Spirit, guide my thoughts and my words this day. Allow me not to stand in the way of the Holy Spirit in this hallowed hall. I want what is best for your house, Lord. Teach me this day what I should do, and I will give you the glory of today's events. Let me be mindful of the needs of every member that seeks your face in these hallowed walls. As they search for your wisdom, I pray that I may decrease so that you may increase."

As the cars began to arrive, we made our way into the familiar church and took our normal positions. I was ready to make my announcement before my usual teaching during the Sunday school hour. Many people waited to hear how my trip to Atlanta went. I could see by their faces that each one knew that something was different about their pastor. There were smiles on these familiar faces as they took their seats and looked eagerly over in my direction.

As I stood up and walked toward the podium, I felt as though the journey was many steps longer than I ever thought before. It felt as though I was standing behind the pulpit for several minutes before I could gather enough air in my lungs to push out the words I felt the Lord would have me to say. Quietness fell over the small church as I began to speak.

"The man you sent to Atlanta last week never returned home to Missouri. His heart was broken, and he felt terribly confused about the calling on his life. While he was in a Promise Keepers meeting, he met his personal dragon that he never thought he would ever have to face. The dragon tore his very flesh and wanted him dead. This dragon made me aware of all my shortcomings when it came to leading a body of believers such as you. As your pastor, I sought the Lord God for a new indwelling of the Holy Spirit to slay this feeling of inadequacy. The Lord heard my prayers and sent many men to bring me back from the brink of extinction and into a new level I am a new man that has seen his true purpose in the Lord." Their eyes never left the familiar man behind the pulpit. I started to recount some of the many events that took place while I was away from the sheepfold. I told them how the Lord revealed himself to me in a fashion that was undeniably God.

As I began to expound on how the Lord had revealed to me that I fell far short of the mark of a good pastor, I looked upon the many faces that seemed not to understand what I was trying to say. The words came forth that I was actually submitting my resignation as their pastor because I felt that I have mismanaged the sacred office I held. Now it was time for them to decide if I could ever measure up to their idea of what a good pastor for this church should be.

As I spoke, I watched as some of the men in the church as they leaned forward as though they could not hear what I was saying. There were looks of unbelief and bewilderment. I thought I was making sense to them, but perhaps I was missing the mark and needed to explain even fuller. I offered to allow some time to pass if they needed to contemplate this drastic move. I could understand if they needed some time to think about the proposition that I made. I offered to stay on until they found a suitable replacement.

I heard some murmuring from the back of the church when John Buchanan, one of the longest termed elders of the church, spoke out, "I don't think we could ever find a better pastor than the one we have right now. I have learned more in the last five years in this church than all the forty-some years before you came here, Pastor Dan. I know I don't speak much in church, but you have made the Bible come alive to this country boy. You have a way of explaining the word of God to me that I can take to my job and my home. I don't believe I want you to step down as pastor."

About this time, Clyde Sanders spoke up, "Maybe we never told you just how much we appreciate all you done for us, Dan. But we really believe that the Good Lord has placed you here for our benefit. It would be an awful shame to see you quit before the Lord says the race is done."

Now it was time for the third elder Bob Cook to make his statement. "I believe the three of us elders speak for the whole church, we cannot accept your resignation. You are the man that needs to be behind that pulpit. We believe God has given you insight to our needs, and we will do our best to support you in your efforts. We may not always be the best of congregation either, but together we can make a difference for God."

As I looked out amongst the many faces of the people I came to love and considered family, I could see many tears and many smiles.

This was something that I felt in my heart would confirm that I was at the right spot for this season of my life. They actually expressed love to me and what the Lord had revealed to me. These people wanted me to stay and continue the work that we started five years ago.

The next event would be an illustration that the new man was behind the pulpit and planned on staying as long as God directed me. I asked my wife—Donna—and my daughter, Lynsey Ann, to come to the platform where I placed two chairs close to the front. As they were seated, I brought a basin with water out from behind the pulpit and knelt down in front of them as I removed their shoes and began to ask for forgiveness in front of the entire church for not being the very best father and husband they deserved. Through tear-filled eyes, they both said, "Yes, you are forgiven. I dried their feet and asked them to return to their seats."

As I looked out to the congregation once more, I saw many wet eyes with almost angelic looks as I saw their faces for the first time that the new man was taking charge of their church in a new way. A broken man, but one that has been humbled by the very hand of God

"I would like the elders of this church to come forward at this time."

I dragged up another chair to the platform and placed it alongside the two already in place. Clyde, Bob, and John took their royal seats as a broken pastor removed their shoes and socks. Kneeling in front of each man, I looked intently into their eyes and asked their forgiveness for not being what they deserved in a pastor. Washing their feet with my own tears as well as the water from the basin drove the dragon within far into the darkness of my innermost being. I assured each man that I would strive to be everything God wanted me to be from this day forward.

Each man looked down on their new minister and assured me that forgiveness was not an issue any longer, as they felt they already had the best minister, but now they were ready for the new and improved man of God that knelt before them.

Bob placed his hand upon my head and pronounced a blessing for Pastor Dan's obedience to the unction of the Lord.

Later that night, I realized that I had one more hurdle to overcome. That was the fact that I had lost credibility at my job. I envisioned that my employer saw me as a fireball that is being extinguished at a rapid rate. No longer did I possess the zeal that I was known for.

Later that night, I laid awake seeking the Lords help in allowing me to form the words that would cease my employment from a firm that I had come to expect to be a part of my life for many years to come. But inward, I felt the dragon as he began to stir. He would see to it that I would not have the sleep or peace that I needed this night. He was still attempting to maintain any control that he had and wanted me to know that he was still there, waiting for me to slip back into his clutches.

CHAPTER 11

—✠—

THE LAST HURDLE

Driving to my office was always the same, but this time, I thought of how the next few steps I had to make to complete the cycle that was unfolding. How would the men and women that I worked with deal with the new creature that came back from Atlanta? Would they see the same broken man that left just a few days ago or see a vital man that was taking control of his life? As my mind raced, I could feel the dragon attempting to wake up and stretch forth with fear and doubt as his weapons of choice for this eventful day. His hot breath was with me still, and he wanted to establish himself back to his previous state of dominating my life of despair and uncertainty. I forced myself to plead with God to calm my spirit and fortify my desires. The drive seemed to pass in a lot less time than normal as I spoke openly to the Holy Spirit to give me calmness and peace. I needed to know that the Lord was watching over me and that I was not alone. It was too late to stop now I must complete the mission.

I contemplated the long drawn out battle I would have to encounter with my internal enemy. He did not want to relinquish his position of holding me hostage in my own mind. Seeds of doubt were beginning to take root once again in the shape of fear and doubt. I fought the surge of bile that slowly crept into my mouth as if I swallowed some vile poison that left a bad aftertaste. I prayed for strength from the Holy Spirit. Now I must face this battle and realize I was no longer alone.

I was usually the first one at the office to ensure things were ready for my staff and coworkers. I looked around at my familiar surroundings and the papers that I left on my desk from the previous week. My secretary just added to the pile of unfinished work and unresolved problems. Looking at the basket, I could sense that I had a tremendous amount of work left undone and would need my attention soon. After all, this is what I was being paid for: to make decisions and keep others directed in their duties. Now it was though I saw these demands of my time and talents as though they had very little consequence in my life.

As the dragon began to rise in my throat, I took command and heard the Lord speak defiantly, *This is my beloved son in whom I am well pleased. Leave him alone.* I now felt the presence of the Lord, and my veins were filled with new surge of power over anything that I had to face. Yes, this was my valley of the shadow of death, and I felt no fear to what man could do to me; for I had the presence of the Lord surging through my body. I literally heard myself chuckle in the face of all the papers and messages strewn across my desk; they would wait.

I made a fresh pot of coffee and poured myself a cup while waiting for the others to wander into my office and look into my face to see if a few days away from the war made a difference in their boss's life. As I sat at my desk, I looked through the stacks of papers and contemplated what would take place over the next few hours, as I knew that today may make the difference in not just my life but the lives of dozens of men that came to rely on my every decision.

This was the day that I would turn in my resignation from the job I had come to love, but now I felt it was time to change the atmosphere of mistrust. I knew for the past several months that my supervisor, Larry, did not trust me as he once did. He questioned my decisions on even the slightest detail. He was well aware that the bottom line of the facility I was supposed to be in charge of had been slipping on a downward trend at a severe rate over the last six months, and whatever I attempted to do did not seem to help reverse this trend.

All my efforts seemed a lot more feeble than when I was a vibrant take-charge man of many months ago. The success of my facility was always measure by the performance of every area each manager was responsible for. My facility was losing money at a tune of over a quarter of a million dollars a month. It seemed that this body was bleeding fast, and it may be terminal. No matter what I attempted to do, the bleeding didn't stop. I could not find the right solution to reverse the downward trend no matter how hard I tried. I sat there thinking about the events over the past months that brought me to this brink of extreme exhaustion and diminished my enthusiasm to little more than a puff of smoke that the wind blew away effortlessly.

Some of my hourly employees had left on a bad note, and I could not figure out why. One minute they seemed to be okay, and then the next there was extreme agitation everywhere I turned. I couldn't get a handle on what was ripping apart the family atmosphere we once had. I recalled a man storming into my office demanding I place him in a position that I knew he had no business to be in.

When I refused his demand, his faced turned red, and I was genuinely afraid that he was about to hit me. He then raised his voice and began to cuss and swear that I had broken my promise to him from many months back. He stormed from my office and went directly to the locker room and then off the premises.

Other workers that were long-time devoted men lost their enthusiasm that they were known for. I sensed that they knew that leadership they depended on was now down for the count with not much hope I would ever recover. The dragon left out a quiet mumble, as if to say, "I am still here, and I have torn away your happiness you once had."

My mind turned to God, *Lord, return unto me the joy of your salvation.* The battle within raged on. All I could do was stand back and watch the hand of the Lord deliver me from my torment.

I walked from my office to the plant to see firsthand what state of affairs was in the facility. My mind raced to the time machinery seemed to fail at the most critical of times no matter how much effort the maintenance department worked. As I walked around the familiar surroundings inside of the plant, I could sense an uneasiness that seemed to follow me. This foreboding presence seemed to be watching me, waiting to trip me or stop a piece of equipment as I walked by. I felt unwelcome in a place that I practically built with my own two hands. Surely the dragon had friends in this place. My facility was in severe trouble, and I felt helpless as to what steps I could take to help those men and women that depended upon my efforts. How could I have let this place get in this shape? I lost my sense of pride and accomplishment. I was no longer comfortable with this state of affairs. I decided to go back to my office and wait for my staff.

The department heads began to wander in to get a cup of coffee and see what mood I was in. With each new face came the familiar questions as to how my time in Atlanta went. I waited patiently for the last one to arrive before I announced what I was about to do after tomorrow's staff meeting in the main conference room with my boss. I recounted to each member of the team that our firm was in serious trouble, and I also told them that whatever they believed, it came down to, I was ultimately responsible.

I saw many puzzled looks upon the faces of the men that had followed me into several corporate battles over the many years we had been together. They looked with disbelief that I would tender my resignation just when the place needed me the most. I recanted that I was not abandoning them but merely stepping aside to let someone else try to right this sinking ship. I told them the Lord had made me aware that I needed the trust of those around me, and I could not settle for less. My heart overruled my mind. I would have to fully trust the Lord to show me the way I must go.

"I cannot work for a man that does not trust my judgment or motives. Tomorrow will be the day I turn in my notice. I do so with great emotion. As many of you know, I put a great deal of sweat and time into this facility. Looking around the plant earlier today, I have come to realize that I have let it slip into a sad state. Each one of you deserves a better leader than what I have become. It will now be up to the complex manager Larry if he wants me to leave or stay."

Chris Karleskint, my head supervisor, was always the spokes-man for the group. "Do you think that's wise, Dan? Perhaps you might want to think about it for a few days to see what happens after you speak with Larry."

Then my production supervisor, Larry, looked deep into my eyes, "Do you really believe that anyone could a better job than what we have done together?"

"Larry, I'll answer your question after tomorrow's meeting with my boss. I have to know that he trusts me, or if he simply wants me out of the way for another manager. Some of you know that he has been grooming someone else that he may feel will give him better results in managing this facility. The choice is no longer mine. I will trust what the Lord does in my life from this day forward." My eyes were full of intensity and determination. I felt they could sense that there was no dissuading me from my decision. It was up to the Lord to lead, and I was ready for whatever He had for me to face.

There was a deathly cold silence in that room, so unlike the many other meetings that were talkative and always humorous. My thought went back to happier times when one of the guys played a practical joke on their boss by placing a rubber snake on the ceiling fan so that when the light was turned on, the toy flew into someone's lap. When the snake dropped onto the table, I thought they were going to turn the desk completely over in trying to get away from their fears.

Tuesday arrived, and I could sense and anticipation in the air from each one of my staff as they arrived earlier than normal to see if I change my mind overnight. When each one looked at me, they didn't even bother to ask; they knew that this was my day of reck-oning. They could sense that I meant what I said and seemed to be more determined than ever to see this action through to the end.

The complex staff meetings always started promptly at 9:00 a.m. and only lasted for about an hour. This morning, it seemed it dragged on and on. We went over budget reports, projection of the new market reports, and a host of other details that seemed to be an effort to bring our spirits down for over two hours. When my turn came to speak, I smiled more than I had in many previous months and let everyone know that the team that I headed up was the best in this entire corporation. I agreed that for the past few months, we were in a slump unlike anything I had ever experienced, but I felt that the drive and dedication of my team was worthy of management's support. I did my best to allude to the fact that I had a plan that would bring the very best results we could ever realize if given the opportunity.

In my mind, God was now in control of my thoughts and my actions. I was simply along for the ride of my life. I could sense that perhaps I exuded an inner strength they had not encountered for many months. I was a force that they had never seen the likes of before. I finalized my report by asking my boss for few minutes of his time after today's meeting. He agreed to stay in the conference room for a few minutes.

After everyone left the room, I could sense my heart pounding, and then I turned to Larry and said, "Larry, I want what is best for this company and those that work under my direction. The reports we just saw demonstrate that my performance is not what it should be. I want to make this as easy as possible for you to get things back on track. It is time I came to the realization that due to circumstances beyond my control. I must tender my resignation with this firm. I can give you two weeks to find a suitable replacement."

"Dan, what gives? I mean, what brought this on?" His eyes darted over my face with bewilderment and surprise.

"I feel you no longer trust my judgment. I cannot blame you in light of the results of the reports we just saw. I cannot work with someone who does not trust me or the decisions I make." My eyes stared into his to see if I could detect the truth, or if I would watch as his eyes turn away, telling me that I touched the nerve that he was about to ask me to leave anyway.

"Whatever gave you that idea? You're one of the most valuable men of my entire staff. I trust you and your judgment without question. I cannot accept your resignation on these grounds. You have transformed the plant you manage to a profit center when nobody else thought it was possible. Sure, you're going through a tough time.

But I know you will turn it around. I am confident you are exactly what this company needs for that operation."

"Thank you for your vote of confidence. I will stay as long as we have nothing between our professional working relationship. I need to know that we support each other in all we do."

Larry repositioned himself in his chair as he leaned forward, "Dan, you're a buzz saw. You cut through all the crud and get down to business when the going gets tough. If there is anything that has to be accomplished, I know I can call on you to get it done without any hesitation. I am proud that you are on our team here. I watched you bury yourself in a problem and forget everything else until you've mastered it. I know that you see the numbers and how they have been going lately. But you'll turn them around. I am confident of that." His tone signaled that the conversation was over, and this was the end. Then he looked up again and said, "How was your trip to Atlanta?"

As I sat there looking into his eyes, my mind raced to determine if I was to share what had taken place over the last few days in Atlanta. "Larry, it was the most remarkable events of my spiritual life. I can tell you this much. I will never be the same man that you knew from the past. Thank you for asking. I'll share more with you later, but right now I have to have a staff meeting with my guys in the war room." The war room was our name for the conference room, which also doubled as my office.

"Go get 'em, buzz saw." He grinned at me and nodded.

As I left the main conference room, I could feel a sense of pride and release from oppression. My heart began to soar, and the daylight was more intense than I ever recalled seeing it. I dealt a major blow to the dragon once more. Now he was on the floor gasping to breathe to stay alive. I felt his slink back into the abyss into utter obscurity to lick his wounds and stay away from the man of God that I had become. I faced my fears and conquered the unknown and felt a new sense of confidence that I never experienced before. The challenge that lies ahead was now a delightful game that I relished to start. My mind was spinning with new ideas and new vigor that came through the Son of God.

The long walk back to my office was filled with prayer and thanksgiving for another opportunity to serve God with a renewed spirit. I could barely wait to get started on my new journey, but this time as the copilot and the Lord as the pilot of this life. He was the king, and I was His pawn to be used in a way that all would know that the Lord was my shepherd; and I shall not want for anything.

As I arrived back at my office, I sat down at my computer and recalled some advice a pastor friend gave to me about my facility. I typed feverishly to put on paper what I believe the Holy Spirit dictated through my mind. I wrote out this declaration of proclamation that this plant would be dedicated to God the Father, and nothing but the best would be tolerated here. No longer would any form of witchcraft, division, slothfulness, agitation, and anything that was not of God would be welcomed here. This just became Holy ground, and the efforts of the undersigned would be blessed beyond measure. This was God's work from this day forward. We were about to do some major battles, and we were not about to take prisoners. I left the document on my desk as my staff wandered in and sat at the conference table, looking at my face to see if they could detect how the meeting went. I waited to an extended period of time when the suspense was high. No one spoke a word. They looked intently at my face, waiting to hear the verdict of my last meeting.

"It looks like I'll be your boss for quite some time if you'll have me."

Smiles broke out on each face as they looked to one another with a sense of relief.

"Where do we go from here, Dan?" Chris asked.

"Now we let go and let God. He now becomes the pinnacle for this business to revolve around. He will guide our steps in every decision. I am trusting totally on Him to make this place the best that it can be as a testimony to His greatness." I then read the declaration lying on my desk and placed it face up in front of me.

We are in agreement!
We want the very best for our place of work!

God has full authority over *everything* and everyone at this facility.

We dedicate our time, efforts, and prayers for the betterment of all that come in contact with this facility.

Anyone and anything that comes against those that agree with these covenants will be defeated. Because we hereby resist all that is not of God.

We pray for all who are in authority that they may find favor with the Lord for the benefit of all.

We resist any spirit of slothfulness, any spirit of agitation, confusion, or anything that does not praise God!

We will ask the Lord's blessing on this facility and those that believe in *His* mighty name.

We hereby stand in agreement with one mind and of one accord.

As the manifestations of God occur, we will give the glory to God for a testimony of His divine intervention!

"Guys, I am not permitted to coerce you to follow my example. I am not really allowed to discuss my religious beliefs with you here. But I have never hid anything from you in the past, and I will not hide my convictions from you now. I feel certain that Satan has had a field day here at our facility. He has attempted to rip this facility from one end to the other. I have watched as each of us has lost trust in our fellow coworkers. We allowed this agitation to cause division and strife unlike we have ever seen before.

"I have watched, as men that I believe are the best in the business become slothful and question my ability to lead a group of men such as you. I want to tell you today that all that stops right here and right now. Last week, I met my inner dragon and defeated him through the power of God. He has been using me as the deterrent here to cause such mayhem that he was attempting to get to all of you and those around you. Now I am about to deal the final blow to his realm here. I am prepared to see him defeated for the glory of God at this place.

"Don't get me wrong. I am nothing. But He that brought me up from the depths of despair is everything. Yet I feel invincible, for I know that I can do all things through Him. I am no longer defeated, but I am more than a conqueror. I am a champion for His name's sake."

I turned to my desk and reached for the sacred document that I just finished typing. "This document is here as a declaration of my commitment to God in recognition of His mercy that brought me back from the brink of hell where his legions were waiting for me to slip into total obscurity. I will sign this document in front of you whom I respect and admire. Men, before you stands a man that will no longer take second best. Here stands a man of God with a purpose, a drive, and a plan to see this plant be an industry leader that God wants us to be."

I signed the document and left through the side door to my office, not waiting for comments or to discuss these words that I just threw into their lives. I felt the need to be alone with God. My mind praised His name for the courage to stand before these men and make a statement that I had no idea how they would take it. I thought some of them would think, *Dan really lost it this time.* While others may be thinking, *This is a man I can follow.* Perhaps some may have thought, *He's back, now let's go.*

I walked around a large pond in the back of my facility for quite some time. This was my sanctuary while at work. This pond was about a mile in length and allowed me to speak to God when things were on my mind. As I walked, I prayed feverishly. The familiar smell of the water next to me made me realize that this is where I belonged; here is where I would find the answers that eluded my attempts in the past. Here is where I could speak to God and he could speak to me. Many times I would walk with Chris around these lagoons and voice my concerns of the facility that I was supposed to be in charge of. Now I was seeking divine intervention to make this a place the Lord himself would have a hand in.

When I got back to my office, all my staff had returned to their respective areas. I looked on my desk, and there was the same document that I signed lying directly in front of my chair. Now it contained the signatures of each member of my staff. I could feel the swell of tears begin to fall from my eyes. These men heard the power of the Holy Spirit speak through me. What an honor and privilege to be a leader of men that wanted more of God in their lives.

I now felt a great sense of responsibility to be a more than just another good manager; now I had to demonstrate what God to do to a mere man of faith. This document sealed my fate; there was no turning back and no giving up now. I was destined to be what the Lord wanted me to be. The final blow was struck to the dragon. His power was thwarted with this final blow. It was now evident that I had the support of both God and man.

If God was for me who could be against me?
(Romans 8:31)

EPILOGUE

Several years have passed since we all signed that precious document on that fateful day. Now my mind drifts back to the realization that within three months from signing this document, we began to generate a profit during the harshest of economic times for our business. Another few months and we were leading all other divisions in profitability almost two to one. Within six months, we set new levels of production and profits that remain to this day. Truly a miracle took place because a group of men decided to follow Christ and not rely on their own strength. It started with one then spread to another and then another. Now it is a way of life for each of us and our families. We march forward and don't look back, for we know who is the author and finisher of our faith. We now march with banner lifted high. We march to the beat of a different drum. We stand for Christ.

Bible studies started in the break room next to my office. Men were carrying Bibles within the plant. Often the guys I worked with would ask me spiritual questions or request help in a family matter. I was looked upon as a man that cared for his fellow man. I was recognized as a man of integrity. Now they referred to me as the facility chaplain. I was being shaped by the very hand of God. It was though the Holy Spirit was now allowed to bring me to the place where He wanted me all along.

Now I am often on a stage during business conferences and relate how the Lord gave me the weapons to face my innermost dragon. Oh, the dragon is still within me, but he has to obey the will of my heavenly Father who watches over me. No longer does he raise his head and roars; now he sulks and waits for his opportunity to strike a blow.

But with each waking day, I acknowledge the power of the Holy Spirit, "Yea thou I walk through the Valley of the Shadow of Death, I fear no evil, for thou are with ME" (Psalm 23:4). What priceless words of comfort we can find in these if we only believe that God has been waiting for a very long time for each of us to realize that He is the master potter, and we are simply clay. We must recognize the fact that the Lord will never push His will into your life; he is waiting for each of us to request His help and guidance. Yes, as I walk through the valleys of life, I now realize that they are filled with only shadows of death and can no longer hurt the man I became in Christ. I am a "new creature in Christ, old things have passed away. Behold, all things are new" (2 Corinthians 5:17).

I will not allow the evil things of this world take away what the hand of the Lord has given me.

Each year, Donna, Lynsey, and I would rent a condo and spend a week in Branson Missouri, which was not far from our home in Pineville, Missouri. That same summer, I called Mike Mack in Champaign, Illinois to announce that Donna and I were going to spend a week in Branson and were asked if there was any way possible for him to meet us there. Mike commented that he felt he could get away for a few days with his wife, Sandy. I anxiously told Donna that she would soon meet the man that attached himself to me in Atlanta.

We arrived in their hotel lobby where I saw a tall thin red-haired man with a smile that could light up an entire room. It was Mike searching the crowd for the likes of me. "Hey, Mike, over here." We strode swiftly toward each other and then hugged as though we were long lost brothers.

"Boy, it sure is good to see you again, Dan. I want you to meet my wife, Sandy."

I looked deep into the eyes of what I thought was an earthly angel that was the helpmate of my true brother in the Lord.

"Hello, Sandy. I am so very pleased to meet your acquaintance. This is my wife, Donna." The two ladies also hugged and instantly recounted how much they heard of the other through their husbands. We must have been quite a sight for others to look on as we stood there anxiously espousing the blessings of God upon each of our lives.

"Hey, let's go back to our condo where we can relax a little."

As soon as we arrived, Donna put a couple of pizzas in the oven for all to enjoy. While we ate, Donna looked at Mike and asked, "Mike, what made you befriend Dan while you were in Atlanta?"

"Ya know, Donna, to this day, that puzzles me. I traveled down to Atlanta with a group of guys from our home church. I got separated from them after the event, and that's when I ran into Dan in the line going out of the stadium. Something told me that this guy was different and that I should attach myself to him while at this event."

A look of amazement came across Donna's face as she made him repeat his last sentence about the word *attach*. She grinned a holy grin as she looked in my direction as if to see if I could still see the hand of God still upon Mike's shoulder.

"There was no reason for me to leave my group and seek out Dan and hang around with. I even had made plans to attend another church service halfway through this event. Everything changed once I got to know Dan. The Lord wanted the two of us to see His power, and I believe it was destined from the very hand of God."

Upon returning home from Branson, I received a package in the mail one day. Mike and Sandy sent a framed sentiment that says a great deal to me, "I know why we are friends indeed. God placed you here. He saw my need. We're friends because God let it be. I'm here for you, and you're there for me."

There have been many other trials in my life, but each time the dragon breathes his sulfurous breath into my nostrils, I remind him who has dominion over this life. He cannot have control or even affect this man of God. For I have committed myself to living a victorious life, and I will no longer settle for anything but true peace given by the hand of the Master.

The dragon was comprised by my own hand. I allowed the cares of this world and other people's demands to be placed upon me to the point that I lost control. I became like so many others that took their eyes off God and attempted to correct the fallacies of life I had no control over. I deluded myself in thinking more of myself than what I should.

The gospels give us an account of Christ telling His disciples to get into a boat and travel to the other side. While they traveled, a storm arose, and the men became afraid of the raging seas and wind. Then they woke Christ, who calmed the sea along with their fears. I now know that whenever a man finds himself amidst life's raging storms, we need to call out to the master of our faith, the Lord Jesus Christ.

Now I truly believe that I must decrease so He may increase. I gave power to the demon; now I am taking it back one step at a time. I am winning the battle for my very soul. I will never go back to the dry, barren life that the evil one sought to destroy me. I am more than a conqueror; I am a child of the Most High God.

> *And I saw an angel come down from heaven, having the key of the bottomless pit and a great chain in his hand. And he laid hold on the dragon, that old serpent, which is the Devil, and Satan, and bound him a thousand years, And cast him into the bottomless pit, and shut him up, and set a seal upon him, that he should deceive the nations no more, till the thousand years should be fulfilled: and after that he must be loosed a little season. (Revelation 20:1–3)*